frantz fanon

Emmanuel Hansen

frantz fanon

social and political thought

Ohio State University Press

All quotations from *Black Skin, White Masks*, by Frantz Fanon, have been reprinted by permission of the Grove Press, Inc., of New York City; Granada Publishing, Ltd., of St. Albans, Hertfordshire, England; and Les Editions du Seuil, of Paris. Copyright © 1967 by Grove Press, Inc.

Extracts taken from Frantz Fanon's *The Damned* (translated by Constance Farrington) published by *Présence Africaine*, Paris, 1963 (and subsequently as *The Wretched of the Earth* by other houses). Reprinted by permission of the Grove Press, Inc., of New York City; Granada Publishing, Ltd., of St. Albans, Hertfordshire, England; and *Présence Africaine*. Copyright © 1963 by *Présence Africaine*.

All quotations from *Toward the African Revolution*, by Frantz Fanon, are from the 1969 edition of the Grove Press, Inc., of New York City, and are Copyright © English translation 1967 by the Monthly Review Press. Reprinted by permission of the Monthly Review Press, of New York City.

Excerpts from *Fanon*, by Peter Geismar, have been reprinted by permission of the Dial Press and the Estate of the Author, and are copyright © 1969, 1970, 1971 by Lois Silverman Geismar.

Frontispiece by Konrad F. Hack

Manufactured in the United States of America

Library of Congress Cataloging in Publication Data

Hansen, Emmanuel.
Frantz Fanon: social and political thought.

Bibliography: p. 209–26
Includes index.
1. Fanon, Frantz, 1925–1961. 2. Political science.
JC273.F36H36 320.5'092'4 76-2619
ISBN 0-8142-0243-8

"We are nothing on earth if we are not, first of all, slaves of a cause, the cause of the people, the cause of justice, the cause of liberty."—Frantz Fanon

This book is dedicated to all those who are fighting for the cause of freedom, the cause of justice, the cause of the oppressed people, especially the black people.

contents

preface

It is now over a decade since Frantz Fanon died, but his ideas are still with us. They are as fresh in our minds now as when they were first written—a testimony to the relevance and importance to mankind of the issues he raised.

Most of the works on Fanon to date are weighted toward a biographical treatment. The present work is an attempt at an analysis of his social and political thought. All research, however, is constrained by certain limitations, and this is no exception. Fanon is known to have written three short plays: "Les Mains parallèles," "L'Oeil se noie," and "La Conspiration." None of these has been published, and, according to his widow, it was his wish that they not be. Consequently, I have not been able to consult them. Fanon is also reported to have given a series of lectures to units of the Algerian Liberation Army (ALN) at Ghardimaou, but so far the Algerian government has put a heavy guard over them as a state secret. It is also claimed that

Fanon edited a small bulletin on the Algerian war while he was the representative of the Algerian Provisional Government in Accra. No one seems to know how many issues came out, and all attempts to trace copies of this publication have proved unsuccessful. This study is based on Fanon's published works and other works about him, and it should be read with these limitations in mind. It is very unlikely that my conclusions would have been different had I had opportunity to consult the works named above, since in each case I have an idea of the general thrust of the argument. Hence, my inability to inspect them has not detracted from my argument and conclusions. I feel, however, that it is my responsibility to warn readers of such limitations.

I owe a debt of gratitude to many people who have contributed to my intellectual development, but who cannot all be named here. A few, however, must be mentioned. I am particularly grateful to Professors Timothy Tilton, J. Gus Liebenow, and Alfred Diamant, all of the Department of Political Science, Indiana University, who as members of my dissertation committee read the entire manuscript in its original form as a doctoral dissertation and offered valuable criticisms. Professor Emile Snyder, of the Department of Comparative Literature, also read the manuscript and offered suggestions.

I have also benefited from various discussions with my colleagues, friends, and other faculty members at Indiana University, of whom I shall mention Professors Don Sorrenson (now at Brigham Young University), Sheldon Geller, and Patrick O'Meara. Many thanks are also due to Professor Gustav Jahoda of Edinburgh University, who read chapter four and offered helpful comments. To my former students at Ohio State University, who kept me under a constant fire of criticism that made me rethink some of my views and also clarify my ideas, I owe a debt of gratitude.

I would also like to thank the Research Committee of the University of Ghana, Legon, for providing me with financial assistance to revise and prepare the manuscript for publication. My thanks also go to Paul Affum, who typed the manuscript, and to Barbara Griffith, who compiled the index. Finally, to my wife, Elaine, who read the manuscript several times and made suggestions with regard to style and clarity of expression, I owe a debt of gratitude. Needless to say, I alone bear the entire responsibility for whatever shortcomings the work may have.

Emmanuel Hansen

Department of Political Science
University of Ghana, Legon

frantz fanon

chapter one

introduction

"O my body, make of me always a man who questions!"

Frantz Fanon, *Black Skin, White Masks*

When Frantz Fanon died in December 1961, he was relatively unknown except among his fighting Algerian comrades, a small group of French leftists who had been attracted to his writings, and a handful of radical Africans. Today, in the United States and to a less extent in Western Europe, his name in some quarters is a household word. Even the Russians, who for a long time have ignored his writings, are now beginning to break their silence about him.[1] His books still continue to sell in thousands, and among some black militants and certain white radicals his words have acquired the status of canonical pronouncements. Books and articles about him are appearing with increasing frequency.[2]

Of all black writers and intellectuals he is perhaps the most written about. In Algeria places have been named after him, and in the United States and Italy research centers have been erected in his memory. He has taken his place, alongside Herbert Marcuse, Che Guevara, and Régis Debray as intellectual and ideological mentor of the New Left and a guru of black militants.

Ironically, in Africa, where he spent a large portion of his adult life dedicating himself fanatically to the fight for African liberation, he is relatively unknown except in academic circles.

Why does Fanon claim our scholarly attention? A number of reasons can be given: his impact, his intriguing personality, his life as a model for the black intellectual, and the importance of his message.

impact of fanon

There are specific areas in which one can talk about the influence of Frantz Fanon. He provides an ideological frame of reference for explaining the oppressive conditions of blacks and other nonwhite peoples in a white-dominated world. In this connection Fanon's impact as an ideological mentor is particularly felt by the Black Panthers. Bobby Seale writes:

> One day I went over to his house and asked him if he had read Fanon. I'd read *Wretched of the Earth* six times. I knew Fanon was right and I knew he was running it down—but how do you put ideas like his over? . . .
>
> So I brought Fanon over one day. That brother got to reading Fanon, and man, let me tell you, when Huey got ahold of Fanon, and read Fanon (I had been always running down about how we need this organization, that organization, but never anything concrete), Huey'd be thinking. Hard. We would sit down with *Wretched of the Earth* and talk, go over another section or chapter of Fanon, and Huey would explain it in depth. It was the first time I ever had anybody who could show a clear-cut perception of what was said in one sentence, a paragraph, or chapter, and not have to read it again. He knew it already. He'd get it on the streets.[3]

The influence of Fanon in providing ideological coherence for black radicals is also recognized by Eldridge Cleaver.

> The feelings and thoughts and passions that were racking us were incoherent and not connected until we read Fanon. Then many things fell together for us harmonizing our attitudes and making it possible for us to organize into a political organization.[4]

Marx and Engels have talked of how the oppressed could free themselves by revolution in the form of a class conflict, but black militants have always had trouble trying to relate class conflict to the race question. Fanon does not subsume the race question entirely in class terms as certain Marxists tend to do. In *The Wretched of the Earth*,[5] he declares:

> In the colonies the economic substructure is also a superstructure. The cause is the consequence; you are rich because you are white, you are white because you are rich. This is why Marxist analysis should always be slightly stretched every time we have to do with the colonial problem.[6]

Due to his recognition of the race question, black radicals even of socialist persuasion find more ideological comfort in Fanon than in Marx and Engels. They regard Fanon as being more "relevant" to their particular situation. This has led Zayd Shakur to say:

> They [Marx and Lenin] were dealing with European phenomena and they were concerned with whites. Fanon took it to another level. He set down the dialectical contradictions that most oppressed black people are confronted with in a colonized situation.[7]

Another area where Fanon's impact is noticeable is in providing inspiration for the oppressed and urging them to rebellion and revolution. If we are to believe a statement attributed to Dan Watts, editor of *Liberation*

Magazine, and quoted in the *Chicago Sun Times* after the riots in Newark and Detroit, every black rebel is inspired by Fanon.

> You're going along thinking all the brothers in these riots are old winos. Nothing could be further from the truth. These cats are ready to die for something. And they know why. They all read. Read a lot. Not one of them hasn't read the Bible . . . Fanon. . . . You'd better get this book. Every brother on a rooftop can quote Fanon.[8]

The point Watts is making here is that Fanon's inspiration has provided blacks with the will and determination to rebel and fight against their oppression. It is not only among blacks in the United States that Fanon's influence in providing inspiration for rebellion has been noticed. In Canada, French-speaking Canadians have been invoking the name of Fanon to back their claim for self-determination for Quebec by the use of revolutionary violence. They view the situation in which they find themselves, as French-speaking Canadians forming a minority of the population in which the English-speaking dominate all aspects of social, economic, and political life, as approximating to that of an internal colonial situation. Whether this perception is correct or not is immaterial. What is important is that their self-image is that of a people living in a colonial situation, and this image is shaped into a framework by their reading of Fanon.

Fanon has also had some impact on political science literature with regard to the analysis of problems faced by the underdeveloped nations of Africa. Of the writing about Africa that owes an intellectual debt to Frantz Fanon, one may mention the work of Bob Fitch and Mary Oppenheimer.[9] The authors accept Fanon's view that colonial rule is violence pure and simple, and that "authentic" decolonization can only come about by armed revolution. With this as the basic theme, they try to explain the problems and the demise of the Nkrumah regime, using social classes as units of analysis in the same way as Fanon does in *The Wretched of the Earth.* Another area where one can discern the intellectual debt to Fanon is in the current writing about oppressive conditions of blacks in the United States. Among these one may mention the work of Stokeley Carmichael and Charles Hamilton,[10] and also that of Robert Allen.[11] Those writers treat the black community as an internal colony and delineate the same relations that operate between the colonizer and the colonized in the underdeveloped countries of Africa. They also treat the black revolt in the United States as a struggle for self-determination, in the same way as colonial peoples are struggling for self-determination. The model is taken from Fanon's works.

Fanon's writings have also had some impact, if only indirectly, on African leaders grappling with the practical problems of development. Among these may be mentioned Julius Nyerere, president of Tanzania, who was so impressed by René Dumont's work on Africa[12] that he made it required reading for his cabinet, and invited Dumont to Tanzania to address government officials, politicians, and students at the university. Dumont deals in his book with some of the issues raised by Fanon in *The Wretched of the Earth*, and makes references to him. It must here be added that Tanzania has perhaps gone further than any other African country in effecting social change along the lines suggested by Fanon.[13] The emphasis on the peasantry and on rural development, the goal of socialist development, the insistence on participatory democracy in the single party system, the decentralization both of the government and the party, the strenous efforts to bridge the elite-mass gap and to prevent the birth of a bourgeois caste, and the attempt to create entirely new structures to serve the ends of man are all measures of which Fanon would wholeheartedly approve.

Fanon has also had some impact on Algeria's leaders. In a speech in August 1963, Ben Bella, the former premier of Algeria, declared:

> Au nom du gouvernement je dois affirmer qu'il [Fanon] a été non seulement notre compagnon de combat, mais notre guide, puisqu'il nous a légué à travers son testament spirituel et politique une doctrine qui garantit la révolution algérienne.[14]

One can also speculate that one area in which Fanon's influence can be delineated in Algeria is the emphasis placed on the Revolution as a primarily peasant revolution, rather than one guided and dominated by the trade unions and the cities. Having said that, one has to add that the current regime in Algeria is far from the Fanonist ideal.

subject matter of fanon's works

One important reason Fanon claims our attention as a subject of serious inquiry is the issues of his writings and the way he deals with them. He presents a serious commentary on significant human problems. The question of the psychological alienation of the black man in a white-dominated world, his inferiority complex, the quest for whiteness, the depersonalization, the feeling of hopelessness, of nonbeing, that Fanon deals with are all current problems of people living in the underdeveloped countries. In places like Rhodesia, South Africa, the dependent countries, and even the independent countries, these problems are still manifest. The forms in which they manifest themselves may be slightly different, but they are the same everywhere.[15]

Underdeveloped countries face a host of problems. To mention only a few, there are problems of how to overcome illiteracy, poverty, and disease. There are problems of achieving national integration; of fashioning nation-states out of a collection of different ethnic groups; of transforming colonial economic structures into self-sustaining economies; of preventing corruption and authoritarianism; of building effective political parties that will function as transmission belts carrying information to and from the national leadership; of creating a sense of dedication and commitment to the nation; of building social and political institutions that will enable man to express and to maintain his freedom. These are some of the crucial problems Fanon deals with, which we call collectively problems of development. But Fanon's interest transcends the immediate problems of underdeveloped countries. His central concern is freedom. He recognizes that the quest for freedom does not end with the creation of free states. He agrees with Marx that the state can be free without man being free.[16] The quest therefore leads to the creation of social and political institutions that will allow man to express his freedom. And it is this generality of his concern that gives added significance to his thought. We may disagree with some of his prescriptions or with his analysis, but we cannot ignore the issues he raises. Admittedly, other writers have dealt with some of these issues, but not with the same universalistic appeal or the same dramatic forcefulness that characterizes Fanon's writings.

Fanon deals with the above questions not in a cold, detached academic way but as a committed writer who is anxious, even impatient, to correct what he sees as wrong. For him analysis is not an end in itself. It is important only as a precondition to prescription and social action.

fanon as model for the black intellectual

Furthermore, Fanon's life and work provide a model for the black intellectual.[17] There are a number of works about the black intellectual, most of which make a negative assessment of his contribution to the question of overcoming the problems faced by the black man in a white-dominated world.[18] There is the opinion that he has not played an effective role in helping to alleviate the problems that the black man faces. In this direction Fanon's life and work provide a kind of model for the black intellectual: a man who reflects, but does not allow reflection to inhibit him from social action, and a man whose social action is guided by thought. Fanon was able to achieve the fusion of the role of the intellectual and that of the political activist. He was also able to make imaginative use of what he had learned in Western universities to confront the problems that plague the black man, but perhaps more importantly the problems of mankind.

Although works on Fanon are appearing with increasing frequency, one searches in vain for a work dealing in some depth with his social and political ideas. Most of the literature on Fanon is biographical. Those who are attracted to the examination of ideas often devote their attention to an aspect or aspects of his thought. The attractive themes are violence and revolution. Important as these themes are, to concentrate entirely on them is to give a distorted view of the thought of Fanon. It also leads to the neglect of some equally important themes. Fanon's writing is sometimes obscure, pedantic, repetitious, and ambiguous. A clear understanding of his thought therefore necessitates a study of the totality of his ideas, using the entire corpus of his writings. So far no such work exists. It is to fill this gap that the present work is undertaken.

the problem

The central concern of Fanon as indicated above is freedom. It is in the pursuit of freedom that he prescribes the social and political arrangements for a life without alienation. For Fanon, freedom is basic to man. In fact, he defines man in terms of freedom. As he reflects on the existential condition of man, he finds that man is not free. The question then is to find why man is not free, and this leads him to the phenomenon of alienation. He then goes on to suggest ways by which man can be freed from alienation, and the kinds of social and political arrangements that would provide "authentic" existence for man, and that would enable man to maintain and to express his freedom. The task here is to examine critically these areas of Fanon's thought. In effect, it is an inquiry into the nature of man, state, and society as conceived by Fanon.

methodological framework

This is essentially a work in political thought; it is therefore necessary to bear this in mind when considering the methodological framework employed here. When we examine the whole range of the history of political thought, we find that most political thinkers have concerned themselves with certain definite issues. The emphasis and the way they have dealt with these issues vary from thinker to thinker, depending on personal interests or temperament, or the age in which the thinker was writing. Political thinkers from Plato to Marx have been concerned to explicate, to discuss, to examine, to articulate, to elucidate, or to state certain political ideals. What these political ideals have been has also been a point of divergence among different political thinkers. Hobbes thought that the most desirable ideal was security, whereas Rousseau thought it was liberty; and Plato thought it was the attainment of self-realization. Another issue to which political thinkers have turned their attention is a consideration of the obstacles that lie in the way of the realization of the political ideals they hold. A third point of attention has been the consideration of the political and social arrangements or institutions by which those ideals could be realized. Our inquiry into the political and social ideas of

Frantz Fanon will be conducted along such lines. Thus, we shall ask ourselves: What kinds of ideals did Fanon articulate, explicate, or recommend? What kind of obstacles did he see lying in the way of the realization of those ideals, and what arrangements did he consider necessary to make it possible for human society to attain the political ideals he held? We may probably not be able to locate specific answers to all these questions, but organizing our material in this way is one way to present the corpus of Fanon's political thought in some logical and coherent way.

There are certain points one has also to keep in mind when writing about the political and social thought of a man like Fanon. Fanon was not exclusively a man of study: he was also a man of action. He tried to live his ideas and act in such a way as to bring the ideas in which he believed into being. In this way his life and personality were inextricably linked with his ideas. We shall therefore find it necessary, in examining his thought, to consider the following:

1. the language in which the ideas are expressed,
2. the circumstances in which they are expressed,
3. the audience for which they are intended, and
4. the purpose for which they are expressed.[19]

There are also a number of perspectives from which one could analyze the social and political ideas of Frantz Fanon:

The perspective of political philosophy. Here the central concern is with problems of definitions, denotations, and connotations of key terms, internal logic and consistency, philosophical premise, and the delineation of a system of thought.

The perspective of social science. This approach is concerned with examining Fanon's presentation of history, sociology, anthropology, politics, and economics in terms of basic social science literature, and placing his ideas and observations beside the works of other scholars in these respective areas.

The perspective of ideology. This is concerned with examining the work of Fanon as an action program, that is, in terms of its usefulness as a guide to action.

The perspective of myth-making. This is concerned with his utopian view of man and the creation of an ideal society in which man will be free and achieve an authentic existence.

It is my view that, in order to gain a clear understanding of the totality and complexity of Fanon's thought, his work must be viewed from all of the above perspectives, and that is the approach taken in this study.

I have already indicated how important Fanon's life is to understanding his thought, and we shall now turn to it.

1. Y. Krasin, *Dialectics of Revolutionary Process* (Moscow: Novosti Press Agency Publishing House, 1972).

2. For the literature on Fanon see two bibliographical works: Barbara Abrash, "Frantz Fanon: Bio-bibliography," *Africana Library Journal* 11 (Autumn 1971): 9-12; Emmanuel Hansen, "Frantz Fanon: A Bibliographical Essay," *Pan-African Journal* 5 (Winter 1972): 387-405.

3. Bobby Seale, *Seize the Time* (New York: Vintage Books, 1970), pp. 25-26.

4. Eldridge Cleaver, quoted in Horace Sutton, "Fanon," *Saturday Review*, 17 July 1971, p. 16.

5. For the purposes of citation, I have used the British edition of *The Wretched of the Earth* (Harmondsworth, Middlesex: Penguin Books Ltd., 1967). In all other citations of Fanon works I have used the American editions: *Toward the African Revolution* (New York: Grove Press, 1969. Copyright © English translation 1967 by Monthly Review Press. Reprinted by permission of Monthly Review Press.); *Black Skin, White Masks* (New York: Grove Press, 1967); *A Dying Colonialism* (New York: Grove Press, 1967).

6. Fanon, *The Wretched of the Earth*, p. 31. One black Marxist who has recognized the importance of the race is C. L. R. James. In his *Black Jacobins* (New York: Vintage, 1963), p. 283, he writes: "The race question is subsidiary to the class question in politics, and to think of imperialism in terms of race is disastrous. But to neglect the racial factor as merely incidental as [*sic*] an error only less grave than to make it fundamental."

7. Quoted in Sutton, "Fanon," p. 16.

8. Quoted in Aristide and Vera Zolberg, "The Americanization of Frantz Fanon," *Public Interest*, No. 9 (1967), p. 50.

9. Bob Fitch and Mary Oppenheimer, *Ghana: End of an Illusion* (New York: Monthly Review Press, 1966). See also Tarsis Kabwegyere, "The Dynamics of Colonial Violence: The Inductive System in Uganda," *Journal of Peace Research*, No. 4 (1972), pp. 303-14.

10. Stokeley Carmichael and Charles Hamilton, *Black Power* (New York: Random House, 1967).

11. Robert Allen, *Black Awakening in Capitalist America* (Garden City, N.Y.: Doubleday & Co., 1969).

12. René Dumont, *False Start in Africa* (London: André Deutsch, 1966). Dumont writes with the same candor and honesty, though not with the same degree of impatience, as Fanon. Like Fanon, also, he blames the colonial rulers and Africa's elite for the current state of underdevelopment, and sees hope for the future in the peasantry.

13. Tanzania, however, is relying on political education and not on revolutionary violence to meet these goals.

14. "La Mémoire de Frantz Fanon," *Le Monde*, 27 December 1972, p. 4. [In the name of the government I must declare that he (Fanon) has not only been our comrade in the struggle but our guide, since he has bequeathed to us through his spiritual and political testament, an ideology that guarantees the Algerian revolution.]

15. For an extended treatment of the relevance of Fanon's ideas to Africa, see Guy Martin, "Fanon's Relevance to Contemporary African Political Thought," *Ufahamu* 4 (Winter 1974): 11-34.

16. Karl Marx, "On the Jewish Question," in Lloyd D. Easton and Kurt H. Goddat, *Writings of the Young Marx on Philosophy and Society* (Garden City, N.Y.: Doubleday & Co., 1967), p. 223.

17. The model also applies to intellectuals of developing countries and other oppressed minorities. For the role of intellectuals in the developing countries of Asia, see Fred W. Riggs, *Administration in Developing Countries* (Boston: Houghton Mifflin, 1964), pp. 149-56.

18. See E. Franklin Frazier, *Black Bourgeoisie* (New York: Collier Books, 1962); Nathan Hare, *The Black Anglo-Saxons* (New York: Collier Books, 1970); G. Hyden, "Failure of Africa's First Intellectuals," *Transition* 6 (January 1967), pp. 14-18; Harold Cruse, *The Crisis of the Negro Intellectual* (New York: William Morrow, 1967).

19. The importance of this approach to the study of the political ideas of someone who is not only a political thinker but also an actor on the political scene is recognized by Christopher Clapham, who discusses it in some detail in "The Context of African Political Thought," *Journal of Modern African Studies* 8 (April 1970): 1-13; Raghavan Iyer adopts a similar method in his study of Gandhi, *The Moral and Political Thought of Mahatma Gandhi* (New York: Oxford University Press, 1973).

chapter two

life and work of frantz fanon

To take part in the African revolution it is not enough to write a revolutionary song; you must fashion the revolution with the people. And if you fashion it with the people, the songs will come by themselves, and of themselves.

In order to achieve real action, you must yourself be a living part of Africa and of her thought; you must be an element of that popular energy which is entirely called forth for the freeing, the progress and the happiness of Africa. There is no place outside that fight for the artist or for the intellectual who is not himself concerned with and completely at one with the people in the great battle of Africa and of suffering humanity.

Sékou Touré, quoted in Frantz Fanon,
The Wretched of the Earth

Practice without thought is blind; thought without practice is empty.

Kwame Nkrumah, *Consciencism*

Crucial events in the life of Frantz Fanon critically shaped his thought and work, and, in order to better understand the man, we shall need to examine those events.[1]

Fanon's life history falls into five main parts: his birth, bourgeois upbringing, and early education on the island of Martinique; his service in the French army; his higher education in France and his exposure to the French intellectual left; his work in North Africa as a psychiatrist committed to the cause of the Algerian revolution; his life and work as a professional revolutionary, both in North Africa and in sub-Saharan Africa. It is useful to look at Martinique in 1925 to understand the social environment in which Fanon grew up and the forces that molded his early life.

martinique: social structure

The island of Martinique, where Fanon was born, was one of the overseas departments of France. Together with Guadeloupe it forms what is known as the French Antilles. As in other French overseas possessions, Martinican society consisted of a rigid pyramidal class structure.[2] On top of the pyramid was a small group of whites, called *créoles* or *békés*. The whites formed a status group consisting of native whites and whites from metropolitan France. Small in number, they formed a closely knit endogamous community. In the eyes of most blacks, the whites consisted of a single homogenous and monolithic group. However, small in number though they were, some gradations could be discerned among them. Edith Kovatz has identified three main subgroups: *gros békés*, the *békés moyens*, and the *petits blancs*.[3]

Below the white group was a small but prosperous bourgeoisie of nonwhites consisting of mulattoes and the blacks proper, and at the bottom was the bulk of the black population. As happens in all cases of rigid class structure, those at the top of the pyramid tried to stress their social distance from those below, and those at the bottom tried to stress their social nearness to those above them. The nonwhite bourgeoisie, a socially well-to-do group and mostly city dwellers, were largely in public service, business, and the liberal professions, like law and medicine.

Status coincided, though not absolutely, with color.[4] The small white group formed a reference group for the mulatto and the black bourgeoisie, who tried to emulate it in every imaginable way. They tried to speak impeccable French, since it was the language of both the white upper class and the metropolitan power. In Martinique, as indeed in all colonial countries, the colonizer's language is associated with a high social class.[5] In Martinique the more impeccable one's French, the higher one's status. And one was considered human to the extent to which one mastered the language of the master and approximated to his manners and ways of doing things. One writer has commented on the magic power of the white man's language on the island:

> Disembarking at Fort-de-France, the capital of Martinique, a person having good French or English is whisked through customs, while Creole-speaking blacks are searched for contraband goods.[6]

Victor Wolfenstein, writing about Gandhi, remarks about a similar case:

> . . . *Gandhi had tried to be like the English in order to be a man*; he was unable to master the task and reverted to his mother's Hinduism, thereby arriving at a workable identity for himself. (Emphasis added.)[7]

This is perhaps the most pernicious aspect of colonial rule: to be human one must be white.

The whites, though less than one percent of the population, owned the large firms, the construction companies, the newspapers, and most of the port facilities. They controlled the social, economic, and political life of the island. They were an ingrown, clannish group; and like their counterparts in other parts of the colonial world (namely, pre-independent Algeria or Kenya, or today's Rhodesia), they were hostile even to the whites of the metropolis.

The lower-class blacks, who constituted the majority of the population, did mostly manual work. Many worked in the fields as cane-cutters, or on the banana and pineapple plantations. Some also worked in the sugar refineries or as dock workers, truck drivers, or domestic servants. Unlike the situation in other colonial areas, the nonwhite bourgeoisie of Martinique chose the path of assimilation instead of national independence.[8]

birth, family background, and early education

Into one of these bourgeois families of small-property-owners Frantz Fanon was born on 20 July 1925. Of the father we know hardly anything except that he was born in 1891, worked as a customs inspector, and died in 1947.[9] Fanon's mother was described as a mild-mannered, heavyset woman, who considered herself just another French citizen.[10] A "conventional" family, they were integrated into the Martinican society, even though in conversations the brothers tended to agree with Frantz's analysis of European racism on the island.[11] Fanon's father was described as a "free thinker" and "a Freemason." In Catholic Martinique this provided the atmosphere in which independent thought could be developed, at least in matters of religion.

Of Fanon's preschool life we know very little.[12] He was the youngest of the four sons, and as a child was quite restless and prone to getting into trouble. He was also the darkest of the eight children. Those who are attracted to psycho-history attach a great deal of importance to this.[13] Among the speculations is that Fanon's preoccupation with recognition may have originated from maternal rejection, which Fanon might have interpreted in racial terms. The significance of color on the island is invoked to give weight to this. Preoccupation with recognition, however, is not a trait peculiar with Fanon. It is found in varying degrees among all colonial intellectuals and is a direct result of the colonial relationship, which stubbornly refuses recognition to the native intellectual. The tendency to interpret the drama of Fanon's life as an attempt to solve a personal psychosis is, to say the least, shallow, and I find totally unsatisfactory theories that class all innovators as psychopaths.[14]

Fanon's early education followed strictly along the lines laid down by French assimilationist policy. The only books available were the official school textbooks concentrating on the glories of the metropolitan power and the French Empire. As in other French colonies, the official policy was assimilation, by which the blacks, or a chosen few of them, were promoted to the status of French citizens, enjoying in theory all the privileges of the white man's existence.

Assimilation and French education were intertwined. As a department of France, Martinican students read the same books and took the same examinations as white students in metropolitan France. Their classrooms were decorated with pictures of the wine harvest in Bordeaux and winter sports in Grenoble.[15] They were taught the history of France as if it were their own history.[16] Fanon and his brothers learned French patriotic songs; French culture was exalted to the skies; French language, French literature, French history, French mannerisms were accepted with uncritical adulation as the only legitimate way of life. The effect of this was clear. It made the students develop a deep sense of personal

on the island's city population of 45,000 for a prolonged holiday. Geismar gives a vivid description of the incident:

> The sailors expropriated Fort-de-France's bars, restaurants, hotels, whorehouses, beaches, shops, sidewalks, taxis, and better apartments. . . . The military could afford to order the civilians around. The servicemen were rough too. . . . What money failed to do brute power accomplished. Cafés were immediately segregated: black waiters and women, white customers. In the stores sailors expected to be served before Martinicans. At first, segregation came about for economic reasons: With the influx of military money prices went up and the islanders could no longer afford to be customers. By 1941 . . . the color lines were firmly established. The servicemen weren't going to fraternize with black males. The women were another matter: The white visitors requisitioned them; they considered every young girl on the island a prostitute. Rape often replaced remuneration for those unwilling to conform to the sailors' expectations. The police, used to operating in a colonial environment where blacks were always in the wrong, dismissed rape victims as overpriced prostitutes. In military courts, the navy's word always carried more weight than the Martinican's complaints. It was a totalitarian racism.[21]

This was the condition of Martinique at the time of the Vichy regime. Overnight the island came to look like an occupied territory. The regime came to represent "rape, racism, and rioting."[22] What effect did these incidents have on the young and sensitive mind of Fanon? Did he begin to hate France and all that it stood for at this moment? Fanon was at this time beginning to develop what one might call "political consciousness," but it had not yet crystallized into the anticolonial, anti-French posture it was to assume later. Like most other blacks on the island, he resented the "totalitarian racism" of the Vichy administration. But at this time, he did not link this to a questioning of the whole French presence, nor did he link racism to the colonial relationship. It was a resentment and hatred directed against the administration and the soldiers, and not at the French as such. Since the French soldiers on Martinique had opted for Vichy, and Vichy collaborated with the Nazis, there was a tendency on the part of the black islanders to regard the abuses that came to characterize the Vichy administration as something characteristic of the Germans and not of the French.

It was in such circumstances that Fanon left the island in 1943, halfway through his *baccalauréat* and in the company of two close friends, to respond to the call of General de Gaulle to save France. Their enthusiasm to fight for the French was underlined by the fact that they had to pay their own fares to the island Dominica, where they underwent military training.[23] By 1943, however, Admiral Georges Robert had capitulated under the pressure of the American blockade, and Fanon once more returned to the island. He did not, however, obtain a discharge after the ouster of the Vichy administration, but enlisted in the French Army and left for North Africa to fight for the "Free French."[24]

Fanon left the island in the company of two of his close friends, Mosole and Manville. Mosole was described as a cynic and a well-informed person, who by 1943 knew all about racism and exploitation. Manville was the son of a Martinican socialist who defended blacks in lower courts without any fee.[25] Manville, whose close association with Fanon might have had some impact on him, attempted to follow in his father's footsteps, and while at the lycée he was always taking up the cases of the defense of other students before the higher authorities.[26] Fanon, then, grew up in the company of two important catalysts: Mosole, with a knowledge of racism and exploitation, and Manville, with his emphasis on the need for action on behalf of the helpless. Fanon was to embody in him a fusion of these two: thought and action.

After a short stay in southern Morocco, they arrived

in Algeria, which was to become Fanon's country of adoption later on in life. While in Algeria, Fanon and his two companions volunteered for service in Europe. The rampant racism in the army and the conditions of poverty were too much for them. In 1945 Fanon was awarded the *Croix de guerre* for bravery in action; and in 1946 he left the army with the rank of corporal.[27]

Fanon's experiences in the French army and the war were to have lasting effects on him. In the army he came face to face with blatant racism. Admittedly, the island had experienced racism in some of its worst forms, particularly during the time of the Vichy administration. This was resented by Fanon and all blacks, but, as we have said earlier, in the minds of the Martinicans the Vichy administration was identified more with the Germans than with the French. The French were different. They held the values of *fraternité*, *égalité*, and *liberté*. All through school, Fanon had been taught to regard himself as a Frenchman, and he was quite unprepared for the treatment that awaited him. He realized that France reserved a different place for its black Frenchmen. On the trip to North Africa the white French troops had attempted to "requisition the 'services' of a group of female volunteers from Martinique and Guadeloupe."[28] Fanon was deeply upset by this incident, which raised further doubts in his own mind about the nature of the reality of the black-white relationship and the hypocrisy of the white world.

Fanon also observed that black troops were always sent to the worst areas of the war and were quartered in some of the most inhospitable places. He did not fail to notice that white troops were treated differently and preferentially. They had different rations and more of them, better living quarters, hot water, and other conveniences not afforded the black troops. Racism in the army, however, was not a simple black-white affair. It was more complex than that. Generally, all whites looked down on nonwhites as social inferiors. Among the nonwhites there also were distinctions: like the whites, the Arabs routinely looked down on all blacks; and blacks from the Caribbean looked down on blacks from Africa; and among the Africans, the blacks from Senegal looked down on blacks from other areas of Africa. It was a pyramid of status based on color and one's perceived nearness to the white man. The Martinicans, because of their supposed cultural assimilation, were treated in minor ways as whites; but in things that mattered they were treated like the rest of the nonwhites.

Manville reports on how the black troops were sent back and forth, to and from, southern France. Their classification as Europeans or Africans depended on changes in climatic conditions. The classification and assignment of the soldiers to areas in France was apparently done on the basis of the level of fluency in French and the degree of acculturation. Thus, though Martinique was in the tropical zone, its troops were sent, not to southern France where the climate was warm, but to northern France where the climate was cold, because that corresponded with their assimilated status![29] The white man, being civilized, lives in cold climates, so as the black man approximates to the status of the white man through the process of assimilation, he is supposed to develop the same resistance to cold and to be able to respond to the physical environment of the white world in the same way as the white man! Correspondingly, the Africans, who were supposed to be less culturally assimilated, were sent to southern France where the climate was warm, since that approximated to the level of their culturally assimilated status. One is supposed to be civilized to the extent to which one finds the hot weather unbearable. Fanon comments on the sudden inability of the Martinican to withstand the tropical heat after a visit to Europe:

> They need a minute or two in order to make their diagnosis. If the voyager tells his acquaintances, "I am so happy to be back with you. Good Lord, it is hot in this country, I shall certainly not be able to endure it very long," they know: A European has got off the ship.[30]

Fanon was deeply angered by the record of German destruction of North Africa. He was also touched by the poverty, famine, and destitution in Algeria. Fanon's concern is even more remarkable if we remember that he was aware that Arabs looked down upon blacks as social inferiors.

> Some ten years ago I was astonished to learn that North Africans despised men of colour. It was absolutely impossible for me to make any contact with the local population.[31]

His luck was to be better in the future. It is interesting to note that Fanon did not react to Arab racism in the same way as he did to European racism. In a way he tended to think that Arab racism was part of the superstructure, a reflection of colonial racism occasioned by the colonial experience. He viewed it in the same terms in which he viewed Martinican expression of racist attitudes towards Africans.

In Europe too there were incidents that made him more bitter toward the French. In Toulon he had to watch white Frenchwomen dancing with Italian prisoners of war after turning down requests from black servicemen who, needless to say, had risked their lives to save the French from the Italians and the Germans.[32]

By the end of the war Fanon was becoming increasingly cynical about France and the French values he had been taught to admire at school.

return to martinique and césaire's campaign

A short period of political activity was to intervene between Fanon's war years and his higher education.

This was when he went back to the island after the war to campaign for Aimé Césaire, who was running on the Communist ticket as a parliamentary delegate from Martinique to the first National Assembly of the Fourth Republic. There is no evidence that Fanon was at this time sympathetic to the Communist cause.[33] He was more interested in the cultural nationalism of Césaire and his negritude philosophy at this time. His participation in the campaign activities of Aimé Césaire was very instructive. His brother, Joby, alerted him to the problems of political and social mobilization in a place like Martinique and pointed out to him the flaws in Césaire's campaign in that he never succeeded in reaching the peasants and the countryside.[34] It is significant to note that Joby felt that it was important to involve the peasants in the politics of the island: Fanon was not only to come to the same conclusion several years later but to make the peasantry the cardinal point of his revolutionary decolonization.[35]

With the campaign over, Fanon went back to the lycée to complete his education. This was in 1946. The picture we have of Fanon at this time was that of an introspective, withdrawn, and serious student. It is possible to surmise that he was brooding and turning over in his mind his experiences in the French army. He turned his attention to the study of literature and philosophy, and he studied the works of Nietzsche, Karl Jaspers, Kierkegaard, and Hegel.[36] He was particularly interested in the works of Césaire and Jean-Paul Sartre, and for a while he thought of a career in drama.

higher education in france

In 1947, after the death of his father, Fanon went to France for higher studies. He first enrolled in dentistry in Paris, but after three weeks of introductory courses he abruptly left Paris for Lyon to study medicine, complaining that there were too many "niggers" in Paris.[37]

Such a statement coming from Fanon sounds surprising at first. Geismar gives as Fanon's reason that there were too many fools in dental school. He is also said to have claimed that he could live more cheaply in Lyon. These reasons, however, are hardly satisfactory, especially when we know that Fanon always had the tendency to withdraw from an intolerable psychological situation. We have already noticed this "withdrawal syndrome" when Fanon was in the Army.[38]

If the statement "There are just too many niggers in Paris" is a reference to revulsion that Fanon felt at the disgusting behavior of the black bourgeoisie in Paris, which tried to be more French than the French, then it is understandable. And one can say that, even at this early stage, he was keenly aware of the problems of cultural and intellectual alienation that afflict the black man in a white-dominated world, a theme he was to deal with so well in *Black Skin, White Masks*. If this interpretation is accepted, then how do we account for the fact that with such knowledge he did try to assimilate French culture? The plain fact was that he had no choice; either he had to leave France or stay in France and be assimilated. It could be argued that he sought full assimilation like anyone else, and to support this contention, we may quote the following exclamation:

> What is all this talk of a black people, of a negro nationality? I am a Frenchman. I am interested in French culture, French civilisation, the French people. . . . I am personally interested in the future of France, in French values, in the French nation. What have I to do with a black empire?[39]

As I have argued above, Fanon was plagued all the time by an internal conflict between the demands of assimilation and the need for autonomy, to be oneself, and that sometimes he repressed one or the other. His abrupt flight from Paris could therefore be attributed to the constant reminder that the presence of the black bourgeoisie in Paris brought to him of his internal conflict, something that he was trying desperately to suppress. He thought Lyon would provide the conditions for psychic harmony. He was sadly mistaken in this.

After a year's preparatory work in chemistry, physics, and biology, Fanon entered medical school, where he worked hard to earn the respect of his professors as a bright student.

While at the university, Fanon continued his interest in philosophy and literature. He read the existential philosophers: Husserl, Heidegger, and Sartre. He also read Hegel, Marx, and Lenin, and attended the course of lectures of Jean Lacroix and Maurice Merleau-Ponty.[40] He was greatly influenced by Sartre, especially by his *Anti-Semite and Jew* and later by the *Critique de la raison dialectique*. According to Simone de Beauvoir, what impressed Fanon most about the latter was Sartre's analysis of terror and brotherhood.

Fanon was also influenced by Aimé Césaire, an influence that is particularly noticeable in *Black Skin, White Masks*, with its numerous quotations from Césaire and Caribbean protest literature. While a medical student, he also immersed himself in playwriting, and he completed three works: "Les Mains parallèles," "L'Oeil se noie," and "La Conspiration." These were written between 1949 and 1950. They still remain unpublished, and according to Fanon's widow, it was his wish that they remain so.[41] This was a period of intense reflection, introspection, and self-analysis. Some have called this the existentialist phase of Fanon's life.[42] It should also be remembered that this was the time when he began to compose the essays that later were to appear collectively as *Black Skin, White Masks*.

Fanon was a restless student, and side by side with his studies he was also active in politics. While at medical school, he helped organize the Union of Students from Overseas France in Lyon, and put out the short-lived newspaper *Tam-Tam*. He was always involved in debates, or going to left-wing meetings, or touring worker-occupied factories.[43]

In November 1951 Fanon defended his medical thesis and left for Martinique. Geismar is careful to remind his readers that Fanon starts his thesis with a quotation from Nietzsche: "I dedicate myself to living beings, not to introspective mental process."[44] Perhaps this is intended to underline Fanon's commitment to praxis or humanism. But the question is that if a medical doctor does not dedicate himself to living beings, to whom is he to dedicate himself?

While in Martinique he presented a copy of his thesis to his brother with the inscription:

> To my brother Félix,
>
> I offer this work—
>
> The greatness of a man is to be found not in his acts but in his style. Existence does not resemble a steadily rising curve, but a slow, and sometimes sad, series of ups and downs.
>
> I have a horror of weaknesses—I understand them, but I do not like them.
>
> I do not agree with those who think it possible to live life at an easy pace. I don't want this. I don't think you do either. . . .[45]

These remarkable lines bring out forcibly some aspects of Fanon's personality: his restlessness, his impatience, his hatred of weakness, and the apparent contradictions of his personal life; for it is puzzling that a man who showed a deep sense of commitment to praxis should here place style above acts.

In the same year he went back to France to do his residency under Professor François Tosquelles, who was carrying out innovative experiments in the field of sociotherapy. He was to make a deep impression on Fanon, who worked with Tosquelles for two years during which time they jointly published a number of research papers.

His pioneering work in psychiatric medicine in Algeria and Tunisia bore strongly the impact of this association.

In 1952 he married Josie Dublé, a Frenchwoman whom he had met while at the lycée in Lyon.[46] She was described as attractive and an extremely intense person. She was of a socialist background and helped Fanon greatly in his work by taking down his thoughts in dictation. She was the sort of person in whom Fanon would find both intellectual companionship and also a marital partner. Certain black radicals who have adopted Fanon have been uneasy about the fact of his marriage to a white woman; they claim it was not right and goes against Fanon's position. This is a complete misunderstanding of Fanon's position. Fanon never preached separation or segregation. His writings about the Manichaean world are descriptive and not prescriptive. It is precisely this idea of the black man being sealed in his blackness and the white man being encased in his whiteness that he wanted to avoid. Specifically on the question of marriage he says: ". . . I do not feel that I should be abandoning my personality by marrying a European, whoever she might be."[47] Admittedly, Fanon has castigated the black bourgeoisie for deciding to marry "white." It should, however, be remembered that his objection was not to marriage across color lines *per se*, but to marriage into the white society in order to escape one's blackness. In this case it is an indication of alienation. It is possible to speculate that he did marry a white woman to achieve *lactification*, a word Fanon employs in *Peau noire, masques blancs* to denote the attempt by the black to become white through assimilation. We have already pointed to his personal ambivalence about the demands of autonomy and assimilation; but it seems he was consciously trying to avoid assimilation through such means. He seems to have thought of the whole affair and to have persuaded himself that he was not yearning for *lactification* by his marriage to a white woman, as the above quotation indicates. Unless we can argue that Fanon was engaged in self-delusion, we have to accept his position.

Certain writers have also considered the question of his marriage significant enough to deserve comment. Thus, Geismar comes near to suggesting that Fanon married a white woman because of the paucity of black women in Lyon or as a consequence of his yearning for *lactification.*

> . . . It seems that Fanon fell in love only with white women. Maybe this was because there were few blacks living in the city, but Fanon himself gave a more interesting possible explanation in his first book, *Black Skin, White Masks.* He describes there the neurotic behaviour pattern of a black man attempting to become white through love of a white woman.[48]

Such a suggestion rests on a misunderstanding of Fanon. Fanon was not a man to marry a woman because she was black or white. This is precisely the Manichaean world he denounced in the most strident terms. In Fanon's view color or nationality should be entirely extraneous to the choice of a marital partner. His commitment was neither to a black nor to a white world: it was to a nonracial society. If Fanon avoided black women, it was not because of the color question. Fanon has told us in *Black Skin, White Masks* the kind of black women he encountered in France:

> I know a great number of girls from Martinique, students in France, who admitted to me with complete candor—completely white candor—that they would find it impossible to marry black men. (Get out of that and then deliberately go back to it? Thank you, no).[49]

Again,

> I knew another black girl who kept a list of Parisian dance-halls "where-there-was-no-chance-of-running-into-niggers."[50]

If these were the sort of black women in France at the time, no psychological explanation is needed to account for Fanon's action.

Although Geismar does not cite anything from the text to support his claim of Fanon's marriage arising out of *lactification*, his contention perhaps rests on this passage:

> I marry white culture, white beauty, white whiteness. When my restless hands caress those white breasts, they grasp white civilization and dignity and make them mine.[51]

Although *Black Skin, White Masks* is autobiographical in tone, incidents related in the book do not always refer to incidents in Fanon's personal life. Sometimes it is only the style and not the incidents that are autobiographical. The work is an attempt to understand the world and the black man's place in it through introspection. The danger of using statements in *Black Skin, White Masks* indiscriminately as incidents in Fanon's personal life is evident from Geismar's work. Fanon, in *Black Skin, White Masks* writes:

> A prostitute once told me that in her early days the mere thought of going to bed with a Negro brought on an orgasm. She went in search of Negroes and never asked them for money. But, she added, "going to bed with them was no more remarkable than going to bed with white men."[52]

Although there is nothing in the text to indicate so, Geismar turns this into an incident in Fanon's personal life.

> Not even the city's prostitutes wanted black clients. Except for one Fanon found who confided she wanted him *because* he was black. She later admitted that she had had an orgasm the first time before he had begun sexual intercourse.[53]

Fanon has discussed in detail in *Black Skin, White*

Masks, buttressing his arguments with copious quotations from Mayotte Capecia's *Je suis Martiniquaise*, Abdoulaye Sadji's *Nini*, and René Maran's *Un Homme pareil aux autres*, the phenomenon of *lactification* by marriage to the white woman, or vice versa. It is unlikely that a man so keenly aware of these problems that he analyzes would himself become a victim. Also, we know that *Black Skin, White Masks* was completed in 1950 and published in 1952. His marriage to Josie Dublé did not come till he had completed the book.[54] Geismar's suggestions are therefore extremely unlikely; neither can one accept the suggestion that his remarks are meant to rationalize his decision.

In France, Fanon was exposed to the writings and the company of the French intellectual left. He was particularly friendly with Dr. Marcel Colin, a leftist intellectual who edited a clandestine newspaper during the resistance. Fanon arrived in France when negritude was still fashionable among a number of black intellectuals in Paris. He was initially attracted to it, and he reacted strongly against Sartre's criticisms. Sartre, though regarding negritude as "revolutionary poetry," had nevertheless described it as "anti-racist racism" and pointed out its limitations, indicating that it was only a fleeting moment in the dialectic.[55] Fanon's reaction to Sartre was swift and angry.

> When I read that page, I felt that I had been robbed of my last chance. I said to my friends, "The generation of the younger black poets has just suffered a blow that can never be forgiven". Help had been sought from a friend of the colored peoples, and that friend had found no better response than to point out the relativity of what they were doing.[56]

He was later to recognize and acknowledge the same limitations:

> I am convinced that it would be of the greatest interest to be able to have contact with a Negro literature or architecture of the

> third century before Christ. I should be very happy to know that a correspondence had flourished between some Negro philosopher and Plato. But I can absolutely not see how this fact would change anything in the lives of the eight-year-old children who labor in the cane fields of Martinique or Guadeloupe.[57]

While in France, he also experienced and reacted against white racism and the hypocrisy of the French with regard to their claims to be committed to universal ethical values. In Martinique it was easy to rationalize and interpret such behavior as the aberration of particular Europeans, and in the army one could always argue that soldiers everywhere are coarse and rough, and do not typify the most decent and gentle of the nation. But when Fanon experienced the same things in France, and even from the liberal intellectuals, his reaction was no longer a matter of doubting French values, but a rejection of France and all that it stood for. Relating some of his experiences, Fanon writes:

> When people like me, they tell me it is in spite of my color. When they dislike me, they point out that it is not because of my color. Either way, I am locked into the infernal circle.[58]

Frenchmen could never forget that he was black and different from themselves. Color always played a central role in everything. Again Fanon writes:

> Not long ago, one of those good Frenchmen said in a train where I was sitting: "Just let the real French virtues keep going and the race is safe. Now more than ever, national union must be made a reality. Let's have an end of internal strife! Let's face up to the foreigners (here he turned toward my corner) no matter who they are."[59]

The blacks were never to be part of the French nation, no matter what their assimilated status was; they were the foreigners who had to be faced up to. He was treated primarily as a black man, not just as a human being. Fanon writes:

> A man was expected to behave like a man. I was expected to behave like a black man—or at least like a nigger.[60]

Even in intellectual circles Fanon was not safe from this humiliation.

> . . . More than a year ago in Lyon, I remember, in a lecture I had drawn a parallel between Negro and European poetry, and a French acquaintance told me enthusiastically, "At bottom you are a white man." The fact that I had been able to investigate so interesting a problem through the white man's language gave me honorary citizenship.[61]

Fanon was suspicious, and to his way of thinking the remark amounted to saying that for a black man his intellect was amazing. Incidents of this nature aroused his indignation, anger, and resentment, and he hated France and all that it stood for.

Fanon was deeply affected by the hypocrisy of the French. He was also disgusted by the self-demeaning attitude of the black bourgeoisie who tried in every way to look as French as possible. He was angered by the oppression of man by man, by the dehumanization of man, and by the fact that France was a living negation of the values it claimed. As he was to say afterward: "When I search for Man in the technique and the style of Europe, I see only a succession of negations of man, and an avalanche of murders."[62]

Fanon was entirely disillusioned with Europe and France, and if he had one consuming desire at the time, it was to get away from it. No wonder that he was to write later:

> Let us waste no time in sterile litanies and nauseating mimicry. Leave this Europe where they are never done of talking of Man, yet murder men everywhere they find them, at the corner of every one of their own streets, in all the corners of the globe.[63]

It was no longer a question of appealing to Europe to live up to its proclaimed values. That was useless. He wanted to get to a place where he could search for his own identity and think of a way in which he could contribute to the saving of humanity. The burden now was to be on the oppressed to do what Europe had been unable to do.

Fanon writes: "Let us try to create the whole man, whom Europe has been incapable of bringing to triumphant birth."[64] He wanted a place where he could feel solidarity with those who were contributing to the "victory of the dignity of the Spirit," where man was saying "no" to "the attempt to subjugate his fellows." Algeria was godsent.

algeria

In 1953 Frantz Fanon passed the all-important *Médicat des hôpitaux psychiatriques*, and was offered the directorship of a Martinican hospital. He turned it down, however, and took a position as *chef de service* in Algeria, after a short stay at Pontorson, a small, quiet town on the Atlantic coast of France. Geismar contends that his choice was motivated by a consideration for his career, since Martinique lacked facilities for psychiatric care or research. He uses this to back up his claim that it was the Algerian situation that made Fanon a revolutionary, and that it was not for political reasons that he went there. Renate Zahar, however, maintains that Fanon had decided at the time of his marriage to Josie to work for a few years in Africa and then return to Martinique.[65] If we accept Zahar's account, then Geismar's position is somewhat weakened. If Fanon turned down the Martinican position because of his considerations for his career, i.e., lack of adequate equipment for the hospital, then how can we explain his plan to go back after a few years? There is no likelihood that in a few years the position at the hospital would have changed considerably. One would think that if Fanon was all that concerned with his career, Africa would be the least attractive place if equipment for his work was very important to him. Zahar's claim is supported by the fact that Geismar himself admits that Fanon sought a position in Senegal, writing to Léopold Senghor, later to become president of Senegal, but his letter was not answered. He had known Senghor as one of the people connected with the Society of African Culture and *Présence Africaine*. He wanted to leave France and go to Africa, which at the time was in a state of nationalist ferment. Ghana was making rapid advances toward self-government, and Nigeria was following rapidly behind. In Central and East Africa there was political agitation. In Uganda there was political unrest; in Kenya politics was beginning to take a militant turn: Mau Mau had just begun.[66]

Fanon wanted to be in the center of things—where the action was. We must not forget his commitment to praxis. We must also not forget that Fanon as a schoolboy had heard a lot about the Senegalese, and it is quite conceivable that Senegal still fascinated him and that he wanted to go there himself. Reflecting on his boyhood, Fanon had this to say about the Senegalese:

> All I knew about them was what I had heard from veterans of the First World War: "They attack with the bayonet, and, when that doesn't work, they just punch their way through the machine-gun fire with their fists."[67]

If the above argument is accepted, then it means that, quite apart from a strong desire to leave France, Fanon had a political motive for wanting to go to Africa, and his departure for Algeria should be seen in the same light. In sub-Saharan Africa, due to language difficulty, he could only go to French-speaking Africa; his attempt to go there was unsuccessful, so he went to North Africa. Here he would not have a language problem. Fanon had already shown some interest in North Africans in France in his essay "The North African Syndrome,"[68] in which he argues that in France doctor-patient relationship as far as Arabs were concerned was determined by color and all the prejudice that it entails. Besides, in Algeria, politics was beginning to take a militant turn. Geismar's position is further weakened by his own admission that Blida, where Fanon worked, did not have facilities for work therapy.[69] Why then should he want to go there? His argument that Fanon overcame his political phase toward the end of his studies and set himself up to be a successful professional is unpersuasive. This interpretation tends to regard Fanon's political interests and his commitment to praxis as the restless actions of an adolescent. He seems to think that Fanon was converted to revolutionary violence due to the existential situation in Algeria. It is quite plausible that, toward the end of his medical training, Fanon tried to concentrate more on his studies; but that he was committed to revolutionary violence before his trip to Algeria is evidenced in *Black Skin, White Masks*, where he writes:

> I do not carry innocence to the point of believing that appeals to reason or to respect for human dignity can alter reality. For the Negro who works on a sugar plantation in Le Robert, there is only one solution: to fight.[70]

This he wrote long before the trip to Algeria. Furthermore, Fanon quotes Hegel with relish to substantiate his contention for the necessity of violence in the pursuit of freedom.

> It is solely by risking life that freedom is obtained; only thus is it tried and proved that the essential nature of self-consciousness is not *bare existence*, is not the merely immediate form in which it at first makes its appearance, is not its mere absorption in the expanse of life.[71]

Fanon continues in his own words:

> . . . Human reality in-itself-for-itself can be achieved only through conflict and through the risk that conflict implies.[72]

Again he quotes from Hegel:

> The individual, who has not staked his life, may, no doubt, be recognized as a *person*, but he has not attained the truth of this recognition as an independent self-consciousness.[73]

In *Black Skin, White Masks* Fanon advocates fundamental change in society. Echoing Marx, he writes:

> But when one has taken cognizance of this situation, when one has understood it, one considers the job completed. How can one then be deaf to that voice rolling down the stages of history: "What matters is not to know the world but to change it."[74]

In another passage he writes:

> In no way should my color be regarded as a flaw. From the moment the Negro accepts the separation imposed by the European he has no further respite, and "is it not understandable that thenceforward he will try to elevate himself to the white man's level? To elevate himself in the range of colors to which he attributes a kind of hierarchy?"
>
> We shall see that another solution is possible. It implies a restructuring of the world.[75]

"Restructuring of the world" is the change of social structure and value systems. In another passage Fanon is even more explicit:

> What emerges then is the need for combined action on the individual and on the group. As a psychoanalyst, I should help my patient to become *conscious* of his unconscious and abandon his attempts at a hallucinatory whitening, but also to act in the direction of a change in the social structure.[76]

It is clear from the above that at the time of the composition of *Black Skin, White Masks* Fanon was already convinced of the need for a change of social structure. When this commitment to fundamental change of social structure is viewed in conjunction with Fanon's argument for the necessity for violence to achieve freedom, it is difficult to avoid the conclusion that he was committed to revolutionary violence for the purpose of achieving freedom before he went to Algeria. His experiences in Algeria confirmed a thesis he had already arrived at intellectually.

Fanon arrived in Algeria in November 1953. By then the revolution that was to engulf both France and Algeria was beginning. There were isolated incidents of terrorism that caused the French to isolate the *casbah* from the European quarter and to institute check points everywhere. In Algeria Fanon dedicated himself to his work in the hospital and tried to bring in changes along the lines that were being developed by Tosquelles at the hospital in Saint-Alban.[77] He made a deep impression on his staff, and as one nurse reportedly said, "He brought us into the twentieth century."[78] The impression he made on the hospital staff is borne out by the fact that it was these people who agitated for the hospital to be renamed "Hôpital Psychiatrique Frantz Fanon" after Algerian independence.[79]

The condition of the Arabs in Algeria was far from enviable. A vast majority of them had at first been denied any kind of suffrage at all. Afterward, they were able to vote in a separate electoral college under an arrangement that gave absolute power to the French.[80] In 1945, against this background of discrimination, there were the Sétif demonstrations, which were suppressed by the French with great brutality. This show of force on the part of both the French officials and the white civilian population led to strong feelings of bitterness on the part of the Arabs. Consequently, the Arabs took recourse in militant action against the French. Algerians in France and in North Africa organized the Mouvement pour le Triomphe des Libertés Démocratiques, which embarked on militant action for independence, though it fell short of calling for terrorist activity. In 1947 a smaller group, the Organisation Spéciale, was set up to collect arms and to prepare for armed revolt.

In 1949 Ben Bella took over the Organisation Spéciale and its campaign of violence against the French in Algeria, and by 1954 it had expanded into the Comité Révolutionnaire d'Unité d'Action. This united many nationalist leaders from old organizations that previously had not sanctioned violence. They agreed that armed revolt was the only way toward independence, and the Front de Libération Nationale, a direct successor to the Comité Révolutionnaire d'Unité d'Action, proclaimed 1 November 1954 as the beginning of the armed revolution against the French presence in Algeria. This was the Algeria Fanon came to.

Initially, Fanon collaborated with the FLN. During the day he treated the French torturers, and by night he treated the Algerian tortured. By 1956 this double life was becoming impossible. There was terror all around him; his nurses were beginning to disappear, and he began to feel that he was becoming less effective. In the circumstances he resigned.

Fanon had also come to the view that in a colonial territory like Algeria, characterized by economic oppression, political violence, racism, torture, murder, and inhuman degradation, the psychiatric disorders from which the people suffered were the direct result of the social situation; it was, therefore, futile to treat a patient and send him back to the same environment. What had to be changed was not the people but the social and political conditions prevailing in Algeria.[81]

In Algeria, Fanon saw a confirmation of the thesis he had developed earlier as a result of his observations in Martinique, namely, that for the colonized the most serious problem standing in the way of self-realization and freedom was alienation. This alienation could only be cured by the destruction of the colonial system. In his letter of resignation he states:

> If psychiatry is the medical technique that aims to enable man no longer to be a stranger to his environment, I owe it to myself to

> affirm that the Arab, permanently an alien in his own country, lives in a state of absolute depersonalization.
>
> . . . The function of social structure is to set up institutions to serve man's needs. A society that drives its members to desperate solutions is a non-viable society, a society to be replaced.

And to underline his own commitment to praxis, he adds: "There comes a time when silence becomes dishonesty."[82]

After participating in a strike of doctors sympathetic to the FLN, Fanon was expelled from Algeria in January 1957. Thus ended his short stay.

tunisia

After Fanon's expulsion, he stayed in Lyon for a short time with Josie's family and then left for Tunisia to work for the FLN. He was now a "professional revolutionary." He now belonged entirely to the organization, and the Algerian Revolution was now his life. He assumed whatever role the organization called upon him to perform. Whatever academic and intellectual interests he had were now only relevant to the extent to which they furthered the cause of the Revolution.

While in Tunisia he worked as a member of the editorial staff of *El Moudjahid*, the FLN mouthpiece. Fanon turned it into a radical paper that commented on the social, economic, and political aspects of the revolution. He also published a number of articles on Black Africa and on African Unity.

In spite of his new status as a professional revolutionary, he also taught at the University of Tunis and practiced medicine at a government psychiatric hospital at Manouba, where he worked under the assumed name of Dr. Fares.[83]

Here Fanon did not get along very well with the hospital staff and his colleagues. The doctors resented his innovations and regarded him as overbearing. He, on the other hand, was a perfectionist, and tried to impose on others the same dedication that he applied to his work. The resentment against him from the doctors was such that they began to refer to him as "the Nigger." Things got to such a pass that the head of the unit, Dr. Soltan, tried to fire Fanon on the ground that he was a spy for Israel, because he had earlier taken a stand against anti-Semitism.

> Anti-Semitism hits me head-on: I am enraged, I am bled white by an appalling battle, I am deprived of the possibility of being a man. I cannot disassociate myself from the future that is proposed for my brother.[84]

Fanon's singleness of purpose, his sincerity and dedication to the cause of freedom and justice, stand out clearly when it is noticed that not even incidents of this nature shook for a moment his total dedication to the cause of Algerian freedom.[85]

It was while he was in Tunis that he published *The 5th Year of the Algerian Revolution.* In some ways it bears a close resemblance to Marx's *The Eighteenth Brumaire of Louis Bonaparte.* It is a sociological study of the effects of the revolutionary war on Algerian society. It documents the changes that take place in social structure, social and political institutions, and in consciousness as a result of the war of liberation. In a way, it should be seen as a sequel to Fanon's more illustrious work *The Wretched of the Earth*, since it indicates the changes that would occur in the colonized society if the recommendations contained in *The Wretched of the Earth* were put into effect. The importance of the book for the liberation effort is evidenced by the fact that six months after its publication the French government ordered all copies seized and banned further publication.

In Tunis, Fanon seemed to have achieved a total fusion of the role of the intellectual and that of the political activist. His life showed total dedication to the cause of

Algerian liberation. In his writings the reflective "I" that had characterized *Black Skin, White Masks* gave way to the committed "we," the Algerians.

Another role that Fanon played in the FLN was that of diplomatic representative. In December 1958 he attended the All-African People's Conference in Accra, where he met Kwame Nkrumah and other nationalist leaders, including Patrice Lumumba, Félix Moumié, head of Union Populaire de Cameroun (UPC), Tom Mboya, and Holden Roberto, who was to become leader of the Uniao das Populaçoes de Angola (UPA) and eventually of the Frente Nacional de Libertação de Angola (FNLA). At the conference he argued for the necessity of violence for decolonization. In a report on the conference that he later wrote for *El Moudjahid*, he stated:

> The end of the colonial regime effected by peaceful means and made possible by the colonialist's understanding might under certain circumstances lead to a renewed collaboration of the two nations. History, however, shows that no colonialist nation is willing to withdraw without having exhausted all its possibilities of maintaining itself.
>
> . . . Non-violent decolonization is less the postulation of a sudden humanity on the part of the colonialist than believing in the sufficient pressure of the new ratio of forces on an international scale.[86]

In March 1959, he attended the Second Congress of Black Writers in Rome, and there he spoke as a member of the Antillean delegation. Fanon's internationalism was beginning to appear. Though completely dedicated to the Algerian cause, this did not inhibit him from participation in the Antillean delegation. In January 1960 he also participated in the Second Conference of African Peoples in Tunis as a member of the Algerian delegation. He was seen as the man who could bridge the gap between the predominantly Arab North Africa and the predominantly black sub-Saharan Africa.

Fanon's singular contribution to the cause of the Algerian liberation at this time was to internationalize the Algerian struggle. In his writings and presentations at conferences he tried to project it not only as an Arab nationalist movement but as a part of the whole world movement for the liberation of Africa and the Third World.

accra

In March 1960 Fanon was appointed representative of the Algerian Provisional Government in Accra. At various other conferences that he attended—the Positive Action Conference for Peace and Security in Africa, the Afro-Asian Solidarity Conference in Conakry, Guinea, and the Third Conference of Independent African States at Addis-Ababa in June 1960—he served as the official representative of Algeria. As a representative in Accra, he concentrated his attention on three main aspects of the African liberation struggle: the establishment of a southern flank in Mali through which recruits could be channeled to fight in Algeria; the attempt to recruit volunteers to fight in Algeria, the armed struggle in Angola and the events in the Congo (now Zaire).

He spent much time traveling to present the case of Algerian liberation and to propagandize for the formation of an African Legion for the fight for African liberation. Fanon's work in Accra was quite trying. His English was not fluent enough for him to be much involved in the social life of the people. Even if he had spoken English very well, it is not likely that he would have got on very well with the Ghanaian national bourgeoisie, which was steeped in corruption, conspicuous consumption, authoritarianism, and a shameless display of affluence in the midst of poverty, the very issues that Fanon was to denounce most vehemently in *The Wretched of the Earth.* In Accra he did not do any medical or psychiatric work; his official position as a representative would not permit that.

In 1961 Fanon unsuccessfully sought posting to Cuba. There have been a number of speculations about this. One opinion has it that he was seeking to return to Martinique and wanted to go to Cuba to study it as a model.[87] It is also claimed that he wanted to go to Cuba as ambassador to compensate for an earlier wounded pride caused by maternal rejection.[88] Such an interpretation invests Fanon with a vanity out of keeping with the delineation of his character and personality. The more likely reason was that Fanon was becoming intellectually and politically bored with Accra. True enough, Accra remained the headquarters of African liberation south of the Sahara; but behind the thin veil of political rhetoric there existed among the Ghanaian political leadership residuary conservatism, ideological bankruptcy, political insensitivity, parochialism, and incredible ignorance about, or tolerance of, international capitalist machinations that a serious revolutionary like Fanon would find most distressing. Looking around for a place to escape from such a revolutionary graveyard, Cuba appeared most attractive.

assassination attempts

Fanon's importance to the Algerian movement and to the whole of the liberation forces in Africa is underlined by the numerous attempts to assassinate him. In 1959 while he was traveling to a camp on the Algerian-Moroccan border, his jeep was blown up. There are a number of speculations about the incident. Some claim that it was a motor car accident, some that his car hit a land mine planted either by the French or some within the ranks of the FLN who wanted to do away with Fanon. A third opinion is that there was a bomb planted in the car in which he was traveling. The true story is shrouded in mystery. Fanon was flown from Tunis to Rome for specialized treatment. In Rome there were two more assassination attempts: one when the car of the FLN representative who was to pick him from the airport was blown up and the second when the hospital ward he was supposed to be occupying was machine-gunned. Fanon had had a premonition and had secretly requested a change of rooms the same night. The fact that there was strong evidence linking these attacks with the French Red Hand gives cause to think that it was the same group involved in Algerian-Morocco border incident.

In 1960 there was another attempt to capture him. While a representative in Accra, he traveled frequently to various countries in West Africa trying to open the southern flank where arms and men could be channeled to Algeria to aid the war effort. On one occasion he was returning to Conakry from Monrovia when there was an attempt to capture him. Geismar reports:

> . . . Fanon was informed that his scheduled flight to Conakry, Guinea, was filled. He would have to wait until the next day to get an Air France flight to the same city. His overnight expenses would be paid by the airline. That evening when a charming French airline hostess stopped at the hotel to tell him that the plane would be two hours late the next day, Fanon was suspicious. It was the kind of personal attention he had come to dread—especially after the 1959 incident in the Rome hospital. Revising plans, he and an F.L.N. colleague left the Liberian capital by jeep and entered Guinea through the dark forests surrounding the border town of N'Zérékoré.
>
> Air France still had Fanon, under the pseudonym of "Doctor Omar," on its passenger list for the next day. French intelligence had arranged for the plane to change courses from Guinea to the city of Abidjan, in the Ivory Coast. . . . Despite the fact that the final list didn't include "Omar," the aircraft was searched thoroughly at Abidjan before it was allowed to return to its normal flight plan.[89]

It is something of a mystery that, in spite of all this, Fanon eluded his enemies.

illness and death

Late in 1960 it was found that Fanon was suffering from leukemia. He went to the Soviet Union for medical treatment, and the Russians advised him to go to the United States, where the best center for the cure of leukemia was the National Institutes of Health in Bethesda, Maryland. But he could not bring himself to go to the "nation of lynchers." He refused to allow the fact of his illness to dampen his activity. The treatment he had in the Soviet Union gave him relief for some time, and he returned to Accra and threw himself furiously into his work. He began to plan projects as if nothing unusual existed.

By May 1961 Fanon was working on the last chapter of *The Wretched of the Earth*. As Geismar describes it, it was "a ten-week eruption of intellectual energies." After completing the drafts, he went to France to see Sartre, who had agreed to write the introduction. Fanon had a considerable respect for Sartre as an *engagé* intellectual, though not without some reservations.[90]

Back in Tunis, Fanon had a relapse, and his friends arranged for him to go to the United States for treatment. Joseph Alsop, a syndicated columnist for the *Washington Post*, claimed that it was the CIA that arranged for the transportation to Washington, and that the CIA had an interest in Frantz Fanon. He went on to mention the name of Ollie Iselin, a member of the U. S. diplomatic service, who was involved in the whole case. The story that the CIA managed to get information from the dying Fanon has been vigorously denied both by his wife Josie and his brother Joby.[91]

There were some suspicious circumstances, however. Fanon was kept in Washington's Dupont Plaza for eight days before he was taken to the hospital, even though there were vacant beds there at the time. This raises the question of why he was not taken immediately to the hospital, considering the sad condition in which he was when he arrived in the country.

Fanon refused to recognize his illness, and while on his deathbed he was still planning book projects. One was to deal with the extent and function of the FLN organization within metropolitan France; another, a psychological analysis of the death process itself, which was to be called *Le Leucémique et son double*. While he was in the hospital, he received a number of visitors, including the Guinean ambassador, Holden Roberto of the UPA, and Alioune Diop, editor of *Présence Africaine*. Fanon had another relapse and died on 6 December 1961 after reading the proofs of *The Wretched of the Earth*, the work on which his reputation rests. In it Fanon diagnoses the ills of Africa and the Third World. He argues that there had been no effective decolonization in Africa because the colonial structures had not been destroyed. What happened at independence was the Africanization of colonialism. There could be no effective decolonization and consequently no freedom so long as the colonial structures persisted; and to destroy colonialism effectively, violence was indespensable. Violence destroys not only the formal structures of colonial rule but also the alienated consciousness that colonial rule has planted in the mind of the native. Unlike the so-called dispassionate native intellectuals he is not content with a mere description of the structure of politics or a catalogue of colonial injustices. He propounds a theory of social action and makes a passionate plea for revolutionary decolonization and the creation of a free society in which man would acquire authentic existence. His vision of the ideal society was that of a socialist populist democracy, a combination of Marx and Rousseau, in which man would be free to maintain and express his nature.

After his death a collection of some of the editorials he wrote for *El Moudjahid* and some of his presentations at international conferences were published collectively as *Toward the African Revolution*.

portrait

The portrait that emerges from this is that Frantz Fanon was a man of considerable courage, sincerity, and willpower. He was a very sensitive person who dedicated his life to bringing about the end of oppression. His whole life was devoted to the cause of human freedom. He was a man of keen intellect and revolutionary zeal. Simone de Beauvoir described his intellect as "razor sharp." He was one for whom the role of the intellectual and that of the political activist posed no contradictions.

Peter Worsley, in a vivid description of his encounter with Fanon, gives us an insight into his qualities and personality:

> In 1960, I attended the All-Africa People's Congress in Accra, Ghana. The proceedings consisted mainly of speeches by leaders of African nationalism from all over the continent, few of whom said anything notable. When, therefore, the representative of the Algerian Revolutionary Provisional Government, their Ambassador to Ghana, stood up to speak I prepared myself for an address by a diplomat—not usually an experience to set the pulses racing. I found myself electrified by a contribution that was remarkable not only for its analytical power, but delivered, too, with a passion and brilliance that is all too rare. I discovered that the Ambassador was a man named Frantz Fanon. At one point during his talk he appeared almost to break down. I asked him afterwards what had happened. He replied that he had suddenly felt emotionally overcome at the thought that he had to stand there, before the assembled representatives of African nationalist movements, to try and persuade them that the Algerian cause was important, at a time when men were dying and being tortured in his country for a cause whose justice ought to command automatic support from rational and progressive human beings.[92]

Like all revolutionaries Fanon was sometimes impatient, brusque, and arrogant toward people whose commitment never went beyond the talking stage. He also tried to impose on others the same discipline that he imposed on himself, people who perhaps by temperament and constitution were not fit for the arduous tasks to which he subjected himself.

Aimé Césaire, his one-time teacher, in a tribute to Fanon goes farther than anyone in delineating his character, qualities, and personality. He writes:

> If the word "commitment" has any meaning, it was with Fanon that it acquired significance. A violent one, they said. And it is true that Fanon instituted himself as a theorist of violence, the only arm of the colonized that can be used against colonialist barbarity.
>
> But his violence, and this is not paradoxical, was that of the non-violent. By this I mean the violence of justice, of purity and of intransigence. This must be understood about him: his revolt was ethical, and his endeavour generous. He did not simply adhere to a cause. He gave himself to it. Completely, without reserve. Wholeheartedly. In him resided the absoluteness of passion. . . .
>
> A theorist of violence, perhaps, but even more of action. By hatred of talkativeness. By hatred of compromise. By hatred of cowardliness. No one was more respectful of thought than he, and more responsible in face of his own thought, nor more exacting towards life, which he could not imagine in terms other than of thought transformed into action.[93]

It is clear from the portrait above that simplistic interpretations of Fanon as "apostle of violence," "glorifier of violence," "apologist for violence," "prisoner of hate," should be rejected. Fanon was a great humanist. It was in the name of man that he rose up against oppression; it was in the name of man that he fought against degradation; and it was in the name of man that he affirmed the dignity of man. If Fanon was a prisoner, he was a prisoner of a cause—the cause of the people, the cause of freedom. In a letter he wrote to Roger Tayed, one of his friends, just before he died, he said:

> We are nothing on earth if we are not, first of all, slaves of a cause, the cause of the people, the cause of justice, the cause of liberty.[94]

Ché Guevara once said: "Let me say at the risk of seeming ridiculous that the true revolutionary is guided by great feelings of love." This we can say of Frantz Fanon.

1. The biographical sources on Fanon are: Peter Geismar, *Fanon* (New York: Dial Press, 1971); Peter Geismar, "A Biographical Sketch," *Monthly Review* 21 (May 1969): 22-30; David Caute, *Fanon* (London: Fontana/Collins, 1970); Irene Gendzier, *Frantz Fanon: A Critical Study* (New York: Pantheon Books, 1973); Renate Zahar, *L'Oeuvre de Frantz Fanon* (Paris: Maspéro, 1970); Simone de Beauvoir, *Force of Circumstance* (New York: G. P. Putnam's Sons, 1964); Horace Sutton, "Fanon," *Saturday Review*, 17 July 1971, pp. 16-19, 59-60; Sanche De Gramant, "Frantz Fanon: The Prophet Scorned," *Horizon* 14 (Winter 1972): 33-37; Pierre Bouvier, *Fanon* (Paris: Editions Universitaires, 1971); François Bundy, "Frantz Fanon," *Encounter* 53 (August 1974): 25-29; Frantz Fanon, *Black Skin, White Masks*; Emmanuel Hansen, "Frantz Fanon: Portrait of a Revolutionary Intellectual," *Transition*, No. 46 (October/December, 1974), pp. 25-36.

2. For a detailed description of the life, politics, and social structure of Martinique, see Geismar, *Fanon*, pp. 5-28; Arvin Murch, *Black Frenchmen: The Political Integration of the French Antilles* (Cambridge, Mass.: Schenkman Publishing Co., 1971); Emanuel de Kadt, ed., *Patterns of Foreign Influence in the Caribbean* (London: Oxford University Press, 1972), pp. 81-102; Jean Lacouture, "Comment peut-on être Antillais?", *Le Monde*, 27 August 1970; Bouvier, *Fanon*, pp. 13-18; Brian Weinstein, *Eboué* (New York: Oxford University Press, 1972).

3. Edith Kovatz, *Mariage et cohésion sociale chez les blancs créoles de la Martinique* (M.A. thesis, University of Montreal, 1964), pp. 49 ff., quoted in Murch, *Black Frenchmen*, p. 15.

4. For a detailed description of class, color, and status on the island, see David Lowenthal, "Race and Color in the West Indies," *Daedalus*, Spring 1967. See also Philip Mason, *Patterns of Dominance* (London: Oxford University Press, 1971), pp. 274-303.

5. See also Pierre van den Berghe, "European Languages and Black Mandarins," *Transition* 7 (December/January 1968): 19-23.

6. Geismar, *Fanon*, p. 6.

7. Victor Wolfenstein, *The Revolutionary Personality* (Princeton, N.J.: Princeton University Press, 1971), p. 208.

8. There has been agitation from certain sections of the population for independence. Fanon's elder brother, Joby, was identified with one of these groups, and as a result he has been exiled from the island of his birth. See Geismar, *Fanon*, p. 11.

9. Zahar, *L'Oeuvre de Frantz Fanon*, p. 5.

10. Geismar, *Fanon*, p. 8.

11. Ibid., p. 11.

12. Fanon went to the lycée Schoelcher between the years 1939-43. Aimé Césaire was one of his teachers, and his influence on Fanon is easily discernible, especially in *Black Skin, White Masks*.

13. Gendzier, *Frantz Fanon*, pp. 10-11.

14. Albert Memmi is particularly noticeable in his attempt to explain the drama of Fanon's life as an attempt to solve a personal psychosis; see his "La Vie impossible de Frantz Fanon," *Esprit*, September 1971, pp. 248-73. For the tendency to regard innovators as psychopaths, see Lewis S. Feuer, *Marx and the Intellectuals* (New York: Doubleday, Anchor Books, 1969), p. 51.

15. Geismar, *Fanon*, p. 15.

16. Ibid.
17. Fanon, *Black Skin, White Masks*, p. 191.
18. Ibid., p. 148.
19. Ibid., p. 191.
20. Zahar, *L'Oeuvre de Frantz Fanon*, p. 5.
21. Geismar, *Fanon*, pp. 22-23.
22. Ibid., p. 24.
23. Ibid., p. 25.
24. It is interesting to note that it was another West Indian, Felix Eboué, a native of French Guyana who rose to be acting governor of Martinique, the first black governor of Chad, and later governor-general of French Equatorial Africa, who was the first to offer General De Gaulle the Chad as a base for the "Free French" to fight against the Nazis. For the full story see Weinstein, *Eboué*.
25. Geismar, *Fanon*, p. 30.
26. Ibid.
27. Ironically, the award was made by Colonel Raoul Salan, who was to become commander in chief of the French army in Algeria and later chief of the Organisation de l'Armée Secrète, a group of army officers bitterly opposed to the granting of independence to Algeria.
28. Geismar, *Fanon*, p. 31.
29. Ibid., p. 38.
30. Fanon, *Black Skin, White Masks*, p. 37.
31. Ibid., p. 102.
32. Geismar, *Fanon*, pp. 38-39.
33. In an earlier article, "A Biographical Sketch," Geismar calls Fanon a "Marxist" (p. 22). In *Fanon* he says Fanon became a communist through joining the Algerian Revolution (p. 19). This is hardly supportable. Fanon's position approximates more to what one would identify as the New Left.
34. Geismar, *Fanon*, p. 41.
35. Fanon, *The Wretched of the Earth*.
36. Geismar, *Fanon*, p. 43. Zahar, however, claims that Fanon took up these studies after his departure for Lyon (*L'Oeuvre de Frantz Fanon*, p. 6). One has to note, however, that in the French lycée the final year is devoted to the study of philosophy, and that Fanon might have been introduced to Hegel, Nietzsche, and Jaspers.
37. Geismar, *Fanon*, p. 43. Irene Gendzier, who also interviewed Manville, uses the word "blacks." We do not know the French word that Manville used in his conversations with Peter Geismar and Irene Gendzier. The French use "noir" or "nègre" to refer to blacks and do not seem to make any distinction between them. American translators use "black" or "Negro" for "noir." Sometimes in the same text where the French uses "noir," the American translation uses "Negro" and "black": "Le Noir a deux dimensions. L'une avec son congenère, l'autre avec le Blanc. Un Noir se comporte différement avec un Blanc et avec un autre Noir" (*Peau noire, masques blancs* [Paris: Editions du Seuil, 1965], p. 33). The English translation by Charles Lam Markmann reads: "The Black man has two dimensions. One with his fellows, the other with the white man. A Negro behaves differently with a white man and with another Negro (*Black Skin, White Masks*, p. 17). For "nègre" American translators use "nigger."

38. This tendency to withdraw from an intolerable situation seems to have characterized Fanon all his life. When Martinique fell to the Vichy forces, he "withdrew" from the island by enlisting in the French army; while in North Africa, he "withdrew" by volunteering for service in Europe; in Paris he "withdrew" to Lyon; from Lyon he "withdrew" to Algeria; in Accra he wanted to "withdraw" by asking for a diplomatic post to Cuba. This shows his restlessness. However, for a man committed to praxis it is rather difficult to explain.

39. Fanon, *Black Skin, White Masks*, p. 203.

40. Merleau-Ponty is famous for his book *Humanism and Terror*, which first appeared in France in 1947 and which deals with violence in a revolutionary situation and the whole question of violence and humanism, themes that Fanon was to take up in *The Wretched of the Earth*. For a full discussion of the intellectual climate in France in the immediate post-World War II period, see Simon de Beauvoir, *Force of Circumstance*.

41. Professor Marie Perinbam, who was allowed by Josie Fanon to take a look at some of the plays in her presence, claims that they reveal Fanon's attempt to solve human problems within the existential framework. They give the impression that Fanon was thinking of the world as a stage, life as an existential drama, and people as actors (letter to the author, 7 March 1973).

42. Geismar, *Fanon*, pp. 49-50; David Caute, *Fanon*, p. 35.

43. Geismar, *Fanon*, p. 46.

44. Geismar, "A Biographical Sketch," p. 24.

45. Geismar, *Fanon*, p. 11.

46. Ibid., p. 52. There are some inconsistencies in the records about Fanon's marriage. Irene Gendzier, in *Frantz Fanon* (p. 272), writes: "According to David Caute, *Fanon* (New York: Viking Press, 1970), p. 99, it occurred in 1953; Tosquelles in our interview recalled, but with some hesitation, that it was in 1953; Geismar, on the other hand (*Fanon*, p. 52) states that it occurred in 1952; Zahar, in *L'Oeuvre de Frantz Fanon* (Paris: François Maspéro, 1970), p. 7, gives October 1952 as the date." To complicate matters further, Philip Lucas, in *Sociologie de Frantz Fanon* (Algiers: Société Nationale d'Edition et de Diffusion, 1971), p. 195, gives 1950 as the date of the marriage. It is hoped that further research will throw more light on this. Since Fanon's death, Josie has established herself as a radical writer in her own right; she is presently living in Algeria and is on the staff of writers for *Révolution africaine*.

47. Fanon, *Black Skin, White Masks*, p. 202.

48. Geismar, "A Biographical Sketch," p. 24.

49. Pp. 47-48.

50. Ibid., p. 50.

51. Ibid., p. 63.

52. Ibid., pp. 158-59.

53. Geismar, *Fanon*, p. 47.

54. I am here assuming that the 1952 date is correct.

55. Jean Paul Sartre, *Black Orpheus* (Paris: Présence Africaine, n.d.).

56. Fanon, *Black Skin, White Masks*, p. 133.

57. Ibid., p. 230.

58. Ibid., p. 116.

59. Ibid., p. 121.

60. Ibid., p. 114.

61. Ibid., p. 38. See also Francis Jeanson, "Reconnaissance de Fanon," in *Peau noire, masques blancs*, p. 213.

62. Fanon, *The Wretched of the Earth*, p. 252.

63. Ibid., p. 251.

64. Ibid., p. 252.

65. *L'Oeuvre de Frantz Fanon*, p. 7.

66. For a detailed discussion of nationalist activities in Africa at this time, see: James Coleman, *Nigeria: Background to Nationalism* (Berkeley and Los Angeles: University of California Press, 1958); Ruth Schachter-Morgenthau, *Political Parties in French-Speaking West Africa* (Oxford: Clarendon Press, 1964); Thomas Hodgkin, *Nationalism in Colonial Africa* (New York: New York University Press, 1967); David Apter, *The Political Kingdom in Uganda* (Princeton, N.J.: Princeton University Press, 1961); Dennis Austin, *Politics in Ghana: 1946-1960* (London: Oxford University Press, 1964); Carl Rosberg and John Nottingham, *The Myth of "Mau Mau": Nationalism in Kenya* (Nairobi: East African Publishing House, 1966); Donald L. Barnet and Karari Njama, *Mau Mau from Within* (London: MacGibbon & Kee, 1966); David Apter, *Ghana in Transition* (New York: Atheneum, 1963).

67. Fanon, *Black Skin, White Masks*, p. 162 n.

68. Fanon, *Toward the African Revolution*, pp. 3-16.

69. Geismar, *Fanon*, p. 64.

70. P. 224.

71. Ibid., p. 218; see also G. W. F. Hegel, *The Phenomenology of Mind* (New York: Harper & Row, 1967), p. 233.

72. *Black Skin, White Masks*, p. 218.

73. Ibid., p. 219; see also Hegel, *The Phenomenology of Mind*, p. 233.

74. *Black Skin, White Masks*, p. 17.

75. Ibid., pp. 81-82.

76. Ibid., p. 100.

77. Geismar, *Fanon*, p. 66.

78. Ibid., p. 68. For a detailed description of Fanon's psychiatric work in Blida, see Gendzier, *Frantz Fanon*, pp. 63–88. For an assessment of Fanon's psychiatric contribution, see Paul Adams, "The Social Psychiatry of Frantz Fanon," *American Journal of Psychiatry* 127 (December 1970): 109-14.

79. Geismar, *Fanon*, p. 68.

80. For an excellent description of political events in Algeria at this time, see David Gordon, *The Passing of French Algeria* (London: Oxford University Press, 1966), pp. 49-79.

81. Black psychiatrists in the United States are increasingly coming to this view. Leading exponents of this position are: Alvin Poussaint, *Why Blacks Kill Blacks* (New York: Emerson Hall Publishers, 1972); William H. Grier and Price M. Cobbs, *Black Rage* (New York: Bantam Books, 1969).

82. Fanon, *Toward the African Revolution*, pp. 53, 54.

83. Geismar, *Fanon*, p. 132.

84. Fanon, *Black Skin, White Masks*, pp. 88–89.

85. Fanon was disturbed by Arab racism, but it did not shake his interest in the Algerian cause. In *The Wretched of the Earth*, p. 130, he writes: "Yes, unfortunately it is not unknown that students from Black Africa who attend secondary schools north of the Sahara hear their schoolfellows asking if in their country there are houses, if they know what electricity is, or if they practise cannibalism in their families." Fanon did not react against Arab racism with the same vehemence with which he reacted against European racism. He regarded Arab racism as the result of European racism. In any case, his position in the Algerian movement would have made it difficult to take a strong line against it. One can appreciate the ambivalent situation in which he found himself when a delegation of black Tunisians approached him while in Tunis to complain that he did not show any interest in their plight. He was disturbed by the incident, and planned to work on the problem after the war (see Gendzier, *Frantz Fanon*, p. 249).

86. Fanon, *Toward the African Revolution*, pp. 154-55.

87. Geismar, *Fanon*, p. 173.

88. Gendzier, *Frantz Fanon*, p. 16.

89. Geismar, *Fanon*, p. 163.

90. Simone de Beauvoir, *Force of Circumstance*, p. 596.

91. For details of this see Sutton, "Fanon," p. 59; Joseph Alsop, *Washington Post*, 21 February 1969, p. 21; *New Statesman*, 30 January 1970, p. 150; Richard and Jean Brace, *Algerian Voices* (Princeton, N.J.: Van Nostrand, 1965), pp. 130–31.

92. Peter Worsley, "Revolutionary Theories," *Monthly Review* 21 (May 1969): 30–31. In 1960 the All-African People's Conference was held in Addis Ababa and not in Accra. The conference Worsley mistakenly refers to as the All-Africa People's Conference was the Positive Action Conference for Peace and Security in Africa, held in April 1960 in Accra and at which Fanon was present as the Algerian delegate. See *Ghana Times*, 8 April 1960, p. 3.

93. Aimé Césaire, "Homage to Frantz Fanon," *Présence Africaine* 12 (1962): 131–32.

94. Quoted in Geismar, *Fanon*, p. 185.

chapter three

political ideals: freedom

No attempt must be made to encase man, for it is his destiny to be set free.

Frantz Fanon, *Black Skin, White Masks*

In the introductory chapter I said that if one goes through the history of political thought, one finds that political thinkers have tried to defend, justify, or explicate certain political ideals. The task of this chapter is to discern the political ideals that Fanon holds, and to discuss how he defends, justifies, or explicates them.

We regard political ideals as the desirable political goals that a political theorist thinks society should strive to attain. The way in which philosophers have dealt with these ideals has varied from individual to individual, depending on the interests and temperament of the particular philosopher in question. Thus, some have devoted their energies to explicating the nature of their political ideals, some to justifying or defending the ideals they espouse, and others have not only defended their ideals but have also tried to bring them into being. The particular emphasis that a political philosopher gives depends on his intellectual posture. Fanon, as we have seen, takes the same intellectual posture as Marx; that is, his main interest is not only to defend the political ideals he thinks mankind should strive toward but also to bring them into being. Interpreting the world is only useful to the extent to which it leads to the changing of the world. As we have noted earlier, in *Black Skin, White Masks* he writes:

> But when one has taken cognizance of this situation, when one has understood it, one considers the job completed. How can one then be deaf to that voice rolling down the stages of history: "What matters is not to know the world but to change it."[1]

The kind of political ideal that a particular philosopher holds depends on his philosophical anthropology. Thus, Hobbes's defense of security is premised on the view that man is basically selfish and strives after his own ends, and that he cooperates with his fellows only to the extent to which it enables him to achieve those ends.[2]

In the same way, Rousseau's defense of freedom is premised on the view that man is inherently good, and it is only society that has corrupted him.[3] Fanon is no exception. His political thought is based on some notion of the nature of man, and it is significant that it is in his first book, *Black Skin, White Masks*, that he addresses himself to this question. Therefore, before we examine Fanon's political ideals it is necessary to look at his philosophical anthropology.

fanon's philosophical anthropology

Fanon does not make explicit statements in his writings, nor does he give a clear idea of human nature in the way one gets from Hobbes or Rousseau. Neither does he premise his philosophical anthropology on any psychology of man. One can, however, build an inferential picture of what he might have had in mind from his writings.

Fanon seems to hold the view that man has an essential nature. We are not told specifically what this essential nature is, but it is supposed to be the same in all human beings irrespective of race, color, ethnic group, nationality, sex, or social class. "I believe that the individual should tend to take on the universality inherent in the human condition."[4] This is the irreducible minimum in all human beings and it is this which defines man as man. It is also the presence of this in all men that creates solidarity among men as men and that makes each person responsible for the actions done by other men. In addition to this essential human nature there is also the existential condition of man. This could be, for instance, the fact of one's color or culture or nationality. A man's individuality is a combination of the universality of his essential self and the particularity of his existential condition. When there is a tension or a separation or a disharmonic relationship between the essential self and the existential condition there is alienation, which is a negation of freedom.

Although Fanon does not posit his argument in historical terms, one tends to get the impression of the conception of man as perfect in some remote past when man seemed to have enjoyed a harmonious relationship between his essential self and his existential condition. Fanon tends to think this condition might have existed in the precolonial society. Man in colonial society does not enjoy a harmony between the essential self and the existential condition because he is alienated, and the source of this is the colonial situation. As Fanon says, "If there is a taint, it lies not in the 'soul' of the individual but rather in that of the environment."[5] This is a denial of any intrinsic human nature unrelated to the environment. It is an apparent contradiction of the position of the essential nature of man. This has important considerations for Fanon's thought as a whole. Fanon's essential nature of man, however, on close examination turns out to be nothing more than man's incessant quest for freedom. This is the universality inherent in the human condition. It is not an abstraction nor is it an idealist position. For Fanon man is completely autonomous. The weight of the past has no effect on him. He is entirely his own creation. "The body of history does not determine a single one of my actions. I am my own foundation."[6] Since this is closely related to the discussion on freedom, Fanon's political ideal, we shall now consider this ideal.

freedom

Fanon regards freedom as man's supreme goal. And the whole purpose of man's existence is to realize this supreme goal. As he puts it in *Black Skin, White Masks*: "No attempt must be made to encase man, for it is his destiny to be set free."[7] Again he writes: "[I have] one duty alone: That of not renouncing my freedom through my choices."[8] In fact, he defines man in terms of freedom. Man is only man when he is free, and man is the only free animal. Freedom, however, is not the only political ideal that Fanon defends in his writings. Nor is it the only ideal he sought to bring into being in his short life. He was also interested in justice and equality. However, freedom forms the central point of his concern. In view of this, some may find it regrettable that he did not spend more time expounding on its nature. The plea that, like Marx, he was more interested in changing the world than in philosophizing about it should satisfy such critics. However, to those who still insist that we can only be in a position to fight for freedom after clearly delineating its nature, we may reply that our limited knowledge of the external world has never been a sufficient reason for inaction. We shall also remind them that the French Revolution gave the majority of Frenchmen a better chance for development than the *ancien régime*. The same can be said of the Russian Revolution, yet if the revolutionaries had waited for a clear exposition or explication of the nature of revolution before embarking on their action they would still be waiting![9]

The above arguments notwithstanding, we can discern two main concepts of freedom in the thought of Frantz Fanon: the freedom of the state and the freedom of the individual. The freedom of the state, which we shall call *political freedom,* implies an absence of external control over the state. It is in this sense that Fanon talks of the underdeveloped countries fighting for independence. He recognizes, like Marx, that the state can be free without the individual being free, and political freedom in this sense merely indicates formal independence. This is what he calls

> a fancy-dress parade and the blare of the trumpets. There's nothing save a minimum of readaptation, a few reforms at the top, a flag waving; and down there at the bottom an undivided mass, still living in the Middle Ages, endlessly marking time.[10]

This kind of political independence has hardly any effect on the lives of the majority of the people. This is what Fanon describes as "false" decolonization. It is merely *legal* independence. For "true" freedom it is necessary to combine both political independence and decolonization,[11] the breaking down of colonial social and political structures and the building of new ones that will enable man to maintain and express his freedom. It should be stressed that even where political freedom is not merely formal but substantive it does not by itself mean that the individuals in the state are free. Decolonization is the attempt to combine the freedom of the state and the freedom of the individual as a single and inseparable social and political process.

The second concept of freedom discernible in Fanon's

thought is the freedom of the individual. At the level of the individual Fanon talks of freedom in two senses: *existential freedom* and *social freedom*.[12] Existential freedom refers to the freedom of the individual in the universe, and has nothing to do with his role in the state or society. It is absolute freedom and has no limitations of either time or space. Its defining characteristics are consciousness of freedom and free choice. Freedom here means both determinism and indeterminism. That is, one is completely self-determined and totally undetermined by one's past history or environment. To underline the absolute nature of this freedom, Fanon writes: "The body of history does not determine a single one of my actions. I am my own foundation."[13] This is as absolute as the Sartrean conception of existential freedom, and Fanon's last sentence, "I am my own foundation," if interpreted in existentialist terms, comes very close to Sartre's idea of man creating his own essence. Here we have a complete rejection of determinism, and a complete rejection of the influence of the past on the present. As Sartre argues, it is not the past but the future that explains the present. But as we have noted earlier, Fanon, though rejecting the existence of intrinsic human nature unrelated to the environment, admits the possibility of environmental effects on man. If I may repeat the quotation: "If there is a taint, it lies not in the 'soul' of the individual but rather in that of the environment."[14]

This total freedom that Fanon postulates means that man has a free choice. He decides what he wants to be and what he wants to do. His choices are conscious choices. If man is free in this total sense, then it means that man is responsible for everything that he does or does not do. In this sense Fanon, unlike Marcuse, would not accept the idea of meaningless choices.[15] For him, to choose is to be free. This insistence on total freedom has more profound implications for Fanon's ideas as a whole than one is likely to realize at first sight. If man is totally free, as Fanon argues, then he is responsible for all his actions or inactions, as I have pointed out above. If that is the case, then how can one hold the colonizer as morally culpable? If one accepts the notion of choice as the defining characteristic of existential freedom, and one denies the possibility of meaningless or unfree choice, then one is confronted with the possibility of being free in a dependent as much as in an independent country. Here the nature of the political community has nothing to do with freedom. If that is the case, then what is the point in fighting for independence? If one can attain or enjoy freedom under any political system, then Fanon's efforts have been in vain. This kind of reasoning also leads one to such absurd conclusions as the case of a "free slave" or being "free" under tyranny or despotism.

Furthermore, if freedom is man's supreme goal and one defines man in terms of freedom the way Fanon does, then death is preferable to "bare existence" (life of the native under colonial rule), since "bare existence" would be a living death. We must also remember that Fanon says he is prepared to risk the possibility of annihilation in order that one or two truths may triumph. These are the truths of the human reality, the truths of freedom. If that is the case, then to risk death in the fight for freedom is justified. The colonized therefore have death as a choice instead of a living death. Such a line of reasoning absolves the colonizer, or the oppressor, from all moral culpability.

In a Sartrean sense freedom is a negation. Thus, here also the colonized has the choice of a negation; he can always say "no." By doing this, he is expressing his freedom and validating his existence. This is the freedom no one can take away from him, and this is what sets man apart from the other animals. It is the capacity, the will, to say "no"; not, however, "no" as an instinctive reaction to a given situation but "no" as a conscious act. It is this that affords the final dignity of man. Man's freedom, says Sartre, is to say "no," but for Fanon it is also a "yes."

> I said in my introduction that man is a *yes*. I will never stop reiterating that.
>
> But man is also a *no*. . . . No to the butchery of what is most human in man: freedom.[16]

There is also one major weakness in this total conception of freedom. If freedom is man's essence, which is Fanon's position, then man cannot experience total freedom because one's freedom will be circumscribed by one's essence, which in this case is freedom. In other words, man's freedom is limited by his freedom. He cannot, for instance, will himself to be unfree.

Another notion of individual freedom in the thought of Fanon is what we have called social freedom. This is the freedom of the individual in society. Its defining characteristics are: consciousness of freedom, self-expression, and obedience to oneself. This is why in *The Wretched of the Earth* he insists that the people themselves should make decisions that affect them. This is something that no one can do for them; decisions should be made not by the leaders but by the people, all the people.

> In an under-developed country, experience proves that the important thing is not that three hundred people form a plan and decide upon carrying it out, but that the whole people plan and decide even if it takes them twice or three times as long.[17]

In doing this, they are obeying themselves; and in obeying themselves, they are expressing their freedom. This is the ideal that Fanon tries to bring to fruition in his ideal polity. For this type of freedom to be realized, it is important that the state not only be free from external control but also that political and social arrangements should be such as to enable man to express and maintain his freedom. The human community must not only be a free state but also a free society.

The assumption underlying the concept of self-expression, or obedience to oneself, is that the individual has the capacity to make rational decisions and that, furthermore, he has free will. His actions are not spontaneous reactions to given situations, but are truly *acts*. Here the concept of freedom is not total. The individual is to some extent determined by his past history and his socioeconomic environment. He is, however, not entirely determined. He has the will and capacity to overcome his historical and socioeconomic condition. Fanon writes:

> Man's tragedy, Nietzsche said, is that he was once a child. None the less, we cannot afford to forget that, as Charles Odier has shown us, the neurotic's fate remains in his own hands.[18]

Here Fanon recognizes the effect of the past on man. The fact of having once been a child is in some way a limitation on man, but the way of escape from the weight of the past lies in man's hands. This insistence on the primacy of man as the agency of all social change underlies all Fanon's writing. It is an indication of his deep faith in man's capacity to change his environment. Although in his later writings, Fanon abandons his insistence on existential freedom—"The body of history does not determine a single one of my actions" —he still regards man as the prime agency of social change. In *Toward the African Revolution* he writes:

> Africa will not be free through the mechanical development of material forces, but it is the hand of the African and his brain that will set into motion and implement the dialectics of the liberation of the continent.[19]

In this sense Fanon's position is close to that of Marx in his "Theses on Feuerbach." The third thesis reads:

> The materialist doctrine that men are products of circumstances and upbringing, and that, therefore, changed men are products of other circumstances and changed upbringing, forgets that it is men that change circumstances. . . .[20]

For Fanon as for Marx, man is not totally determined by circumstances. Man still has the capacity and the will to go beyond the historical condition and initiate the cycle of his freedom. It is this profound belief in man and an optimistic view of history that marks Fanon's writings. It is on account of this belief that he urges the colonized to rise above their historical condition. From this it is difficult to agree with those who see in Fanon a pessimist.[21]

As I have stated above several times, for Fanon man is freedom. But as he looks around himself, he finds that man, and particularly the black man, is not free. The question then is: Why are men, and in particular the black man, not free? This leads him to an examination of the phenomenon of alienation, the subject of the next chapter.

1. P. 17. The voice rolling down the stages of history is that of Marx, and the quotation, which Fanon probably reproduced from memory, is: "The philosophers have only *interpreted* the world, in various ways; the point, however, is to *change* it" (Karl Marx, "Theses on Feuerbach," in Lewis Feuer, ed., *Marx and Engels: Basic Writings on Politics and Philosophy* [Garden City, N.Y.: Doubleday, 1959], p. 245).

2. Thomas Hobbes, *Leviathan*, ed. C. B. Macpherson (Harmondsworth-Middlesex, England: Penguin, 1968).

3. Jean-Jacques Rousseau, *The Social Contract and Discourse on the Origin of Inequality*, ed. Lester G. Crocker (New York: Washington Square Press, 1967).

4. Fanon, *Black Skin, White Masks*, p. 12.

5. Ibid., p. 213.

6. Ibid., p. 231.

7. Ibid., p. 230.

8. Ibid., p. 229.

9. We can make the same argument about the Cuban Revolution.

10. *The Wretched of the Earth*, p. 118.

11. For a discussion of the various senses in which Fanon uses these terms, see chapter five below.

12. These are not Fanon's terms. We have only categorized the terms in this way to make the discussion analytically meaningful.

13. *Black Skin, White Masks*, p. 231.

14. Ibid., p. 213.

15. Marcuse argues that modern affluent capitalist society offers man only a meaningless and illusory choice. See "Repressive Tolerance," in Robert Paul Wolff et al., *A Critique of Pure Tolerance* (Boston: Beacon Press, 1969), pp. 81-123.

16. *Black Skin, White Masks*, p. 222.

17. Pp. 155-56.

18. *Black Skin, White Masks*, p. 12.

19. P. 173.

20. P. 244.

21. Adele Jinadu, "On the Notion of 'Deficiency' in Frantz Fanon," paper read at the Fifteenth Annual Conference of the African Studies Association, Philadelphia, 8-11 November 1971.

chapter four

obstacles to freedom: alienation

I am talking about societies drained of their essence, cultures trampled underfoot, institutions undermined, lands confiscated, religions smashed, magnificent artistic creations destroyed, extraordinary possibilities wiped out. . . .

I am talking about thousands of men sacrificed to the Congo-Océan. I am talking about those who, as I write this, are digging the harbour of Abidjan by hand. I am talking about millions of men torn from their gods, their land, their habits, their life—from life, from the dance, from wisdom.

I am talking about millions of men in whom fear has been cunningly instilled, who have been taught to have an inferiority complex, to tremble, kneel, despair, and behave like flunkies.

Aimé Césaire, *Discourse on Colonialism*

In the man of color there is a constant effort to run away from his own individuality, to annihilate his own presence. Whenever a man of color protests, there is alienation. Whenever a man of color rebukes, there is alienation.

Frantz Fanon, *Black Skin, White Masks*

Alienation has now become one of the vogue words in both academic and popular literature. It is a shorthand word used to describe a variety of conditions. Thus when students go on a rampage and destroy college buildings and ask for changes in the curriculum, they are said to be alienated; when children do not see eye to eye with their parents on social issues, they are said to be alienated; when young men and women decide that they have had enough of the materialism and hypocrisy of modern living, they are said to be alienated; when blacks in the United States react against the oppressive conditions in which they live, they are said to be alienated; when housewives get bored with their husbands' obsession with money and getting ahead, they are said to be alienated; when factory workers complain of the monotony of working conditions, they are said to be alienated. Most of modern society's ills are explained by reference to alienation.

Although the term is used to refer to particular conditions, different people seem to have different conditions in mind when they employ it. Part of the current popularity of the term lies in the fact that the writers who make frequent use of it are those who are at the moment enjoying some popularity and influence, namely, Marx, Sartre, and Erich Fromm.[1] Besides, the conditions they use the word to designate are conditions in which many people find themselves. When it is suggested that man has an essential nature, and that the lives of many fall short of realizing this essential nature, and that one's relations with other men are not what they ought to be, and that the work done by most people does not contribute to the realization of their true selves, most people are likely to listen. This is so when we realize that men are always searching for some ideal conditions of life.

The widespread use of the term *alienation* to designate different conditions of human existence imposes a problem on the writer who attempts to analyze the phenomenological condition of alienation, since to engage in such an analysis presupposes a clear idea of the linguistic usage. Important as this is, we shall not launch a discussion of the problem, nor is a survey of how the term has been used in the classical literature and various other pieces of writing necessary here. There is good literature on the subject, and there is no need to restate here what has been so adequately dealt with by other writers.[2]

We shall, however, preface our discussion on alienation in the thought of Frantz Fanon with some remarks on his use of the term. He does not make profuse use of it in his writings. In fact, it is only in his first book, *Black Skin, White Masks*, that the term occurs with any degree of frequency. In *The Wretched of the Earth* and *A Dying Colonialism*, it occurs hardly at all. In *Toward the African Revolution* he makes very sparing use of the term. However, even in places where Fanon does not specifically employ the term, it does not mean that he is not concerned with the phenomenon. He announces in his first book that alienation is the subject of his study: " . . . The subject of our study is the dupes and those who dupe them, the alienated. . . ."[3] Earlier he writes, "I am speaking here, on the one hand, of alienated (duped) blacks, and, on the other, of no less alienated (duping and duped) whites."[4]

Fanon uses the word *alienation* to indicate a variety of phenomena. He uses it to identify a "psychoexistential complex"[5]—a series of inferiority complexes that manifest themselves in the existential condition of the individual. He also uses the word to indicate a condition of separation or attempted separation of the individual from himself. "A Senegalese learns Creole in order to pass as an Antilles native: I call this alienation."[6] Here it is a separation or an attempted separation of the individual from his existential self or an aspect of his existential self. The fact of being "Senegalese" is part of the existential self of a native of Senegal, and to run away from this is to manifest alienation. In the same way, a black man who tries to run away from his existential condition of blackness manifests alienation.

In emphasizing the idea of separation, Fanon writes:

> In the man of color there is a constant effort to run away from his own individuality, to annihilate his own presence. Whenever a man of color protests, there is alienation. Whenever a man of color rebukes, there is alienation.[7]

One has to note here, however, that Fanon has added another dimension to the notion of separation. It is the notion of "annihilation" of the existential self. To run away from the self is merely to avoid the self, but here Fanon is also talking of suppressing the self and killing it. In both cases alienation is manifested.

Fanon sometimes uses the term *alienation* to designate a condition of neurosis.

> The Negro enslaved by his inferiority, the white man enslaved by his superiority alike behave in accordance with a neurotic orientation. Therefore I have been led to consider their alienation in terms of psychoanalytical classifications.[8]

Also:

> Scientific objectivity was barred to me, for the alienated, the neurotic, was my brother, my sister, my father.[9]

We may admit that a person who has an acute desire to run away from himself, from his individuality, as in the case Fanon describes, will probably develop a neurosis. A neurotic person may manifest some of the conditions we attribute to the alienated person, but it is doubtful if all alienated persons manifest conditions of neurosis.

Fanon also uses the phrase *authentic alienation*.[10] By this he seems to have neurosis in mind. He reproduces the case history of a patient that illustrates this "authentic alienation." But the case he quotes illustrates a case of neurosis. His own quotation from the hospital records reads: "afflicted with neurotic tics that began at the age of ten. . . ."[11] Fanon's comments on the case also read: "I do not want to elaborate on the infrastructure of this psychoneurosis."[12] In spite of this, he concludes: "It is clear that her alienation is the result of a fear of the Negro."[13] We can thus see that he uses the words *alienation* and *neurosis* to describe the same condition.

Psychic alienation is another term Fanon employs.[14] Here he tends to think of alienation in the psychological or psychoanalytic sense. What we must note, however, is that alienation is always a psychological condition. Hence, it is nothing more than alienation in the ordinary sense of the word. Another term Fanon uses is *intellectual alienation*.[15] This is to designate the alienation of the intellectual of the colonized society. It implies a search for, and a return to, his African culture, history, and traditions as a way of validating his authenticity. This interest in the cultures and traditions of the native by the native intellectual is the result of a reaction against cultural assimilation. Fanon thinks that those who have not undergone cultural assimilation do not suffer from this type of alienation.

> The few working-class people whom I had the chance to know in Paris never took it on themselves to pose the problem of the discovery of a Negro past. They knew they were black, but, they told me, that made no difference in anything.[16]

Fanon also uses other terms to designate the condition of alienation. "To us, the man who adores the Negro is as 'sick' as the man who abominates him."[17] Here the word *sick* is a reference to the state of alienation. For Fanon, alienation is always a pathological condition.

For Fanon, assimilation is another word for alienation:

> This event, which is commonly designated as alienation, is naturally very important. It is found in the official texts under the name of assimilation.[18]

Summing up, we can say that Fanon uses the word *alienation* to designate conditions of separation of the individual from his individuality, his culture, or his existential condition. It is also used to describe a denial or a suppression of the individuality. The condition of hopelessness, or the meaninglessness of life that sociologists tend to associate with the condition of alienation, will be for Fanon an outward manifestation of the separation of the individual from his individuality, his culture, or his existential condition. We have also seen that Fanon uses the word to cover cases of neurotic conditions.

Certain writers think that the individual should be aware of his alienated condition before one can talk of alienation.[19] Fanon does not make this distinction. Others also indicate that alienation presupposes a condition of separation where once unity prevailed.[20] Fanon seems to have this in mind, since he tends to think that in pre-colonial African society there was no case of alienation.

Alienation also involves the individual or the group. In the case of the natives of the colonized society, Fanon claims that it is alienation of the group: "It will be seen that the black man's alienation is not an individual question."[21] Here the argument is that since the entire group of the natives of the colonized society is subject to the domination of the colonizers, the whole group is alienated. The colonized group as a whole suffers from colonial alienation. In addition, individuals may suffer from other forms of alienation. Fanon, however, writes: "Many Negroes will not find themselves in what follows. This is equally true of many whites."[22] The blacks who will not find themselves in his study (the non-alienated) are the rural peasants or those who do not form part of the colonial society.

> The "jungle savage" is not what I have in mind. That is because for him certain factors have not yet acquired importance.[23]

The implication is that the rural native has not yet come into contact with certain modes of existence brought about by the colonial relationship that cause the alienation. The rural native is thus of the colonized country but really outside the colonial system or, at best, is only a marginal part of it. This is one reason why Fanon regards the peasantry as the most revolutionary group.[24] They are not alienated. Fanon does not really deal with the whites. He does not, for instance, give us a portrait of the alienated white, so his statement about the whites is irrelevant. To get a picture of the alienated and the non-alienated whites, we have to turn to Albert Memmi, the Tunisian writer.[25]

Not all the natives of the colonized society are alienated to the same extent; some are more alienated than others, depending on the kind of place and the relationship that they occupy in the colonial system. Fanon regards the native intellectual as the most alienated:

> This native bourgeoisie, which has adopted unreservedly and with enthusiasm the ways of thinking characteristic of the mother country, which has become wonderfully detached from its own thought and has based its consciousness upon foundations which are typically foreign. . . .[26]

Again he writes:

> The educated Negro, slave of the spontaneous and cosmic Negro myth, feels at a given stage that his race no longer understands him.
>
> Or that he no longer understands it.
>
> Then he congratulates himself on this, and enlarging the difference, the incomprehension, the disharmony, he finds in them the meaning of his real humanity.[27]

The intellectuals are the most alienated because they, more than any other group, have assimilated, or tried to assimilate, the thought forms, the mannerisms, and the mode of life of the colonizer—a way of life that is a contradiction of their own nature and existence. They are alienated in all respects: from themselves, from their culture, and from their societies.

The peasants, on the other hand, have not assimilated the cultural patterns and thought forms of the colonial masters. They are closer to their own culture, and have a greater degree of confidence in themselves. They know the history of the people from the "authentic" sources, that is, their forefathers. They also know of the heroic attempts made by their fathers to repel the first white invaders. They have no doubts about themselves or their culture or what they can do. They have, in short, not accepted the legitimacy of the colonial regime.

> The memory of the anti-colonial period is very much alive in the villages, where women still croon in their children's ears songs to which the warriors marched when they went out to fight the conquerors. At twelve or thirteen years of age the village children know the names of the old men who were in the last rising, and the dreams they dream in the *douars* or in the villages are not those of money or of getting through their exams like the children of the towns, but dreams of identification with some rebel or another, the story of whose heroic death still today moves them to tears.[28]

The picture that Fanon paints of the peasant is far from reality. It is conceivable that at some time in the past this might have been so; but it is certainly not the case now, nor was it even when he wrote. The introduction of Westernization and the cash economy that accompanied colonial rule have affected not only the life patterns of the peasant but also his values. Through labor migration many peasants have come to live part of their lives in the city, and this has affected their values. The future they envisage for their children is not that of anti-colonial hero or peasant but of white-collar worker in the city. Their children also dream of the exciting lives in the cities. Fanon argues in a way that assumes that the peasants have a static existence. This is surprising, especially since he insists so much on how profoundly colonial rule has changed the character and the functioning of the traditional structures. How can colonial rule affect the functioning of the traditional structures without affecting the lives of the peasants? It is important to stress this, because his view of the revolutionary peasantry is based on this supposed purity of the peasant's life and the preservation of his values.

The native is not the only one alienated; his white oppressor is also alienated. "We shall go very slowly, for there are two camps: the white and the black."[29] The alienation of the white oppressor is caused by the kind of social relations that colonial rule engenders. The relations of superordination that he assumes, in contrast to those of subordination that are demanded of the native, produce in the white oppressor a superiority complex, and this detracts from his "authenticity."[30] Besides, the Manichaean world in which he lives also gives rise to alienation. "The white man is sealed in his whiteness. The black man in his blackness."[31] Fanon's position, however, as he announces in *Black Skin, White Masks*, is not so much to seek to change the white oppressor, but to teach the black not to be a slave to the stereotypes that the whites try to impose upon him. "What is important is not to educate them [the alienated whites], but to teach the Negro not to be the slave of their archetypes."[32]

alienation and colonialism

For Fanon, alienation is the result of a colonialist society.

> The black man has two dimensions. One with his fellows, the other with the white man. A Negro behaves differently with a white man and with another Negro. That this self-division is a direct result of colonialist subjugation is beyond question. . . .[33]

Fanon argues that colonial alienation is fundamentally economic.

> If there is an inferiority complex, it is the outcome of a double process:—primarily, economic;—subsequently, the internalization—or, better, the epidermalization—of this inferiority.[34]

Despite this statement, Fanon does not go into a discussion of the economic forms of alienation. He devotes more space to discussing the cultural and psychological forms of alienation of the colonized native. As said above, for Fanon alienation is the result of colonialist subjection that is to him fundamentally economic. Originally economic, this subjection is later rationalized in cultural, psychological, and religious terms, and applied to the whole native population, which can easily be identified because of its color. Sometimes one gets the impression that for Fanon, the mere coming together of the whites and the blacks creates alienation in the black man.

> I believe that the fact of the juxtaposition of the white and the black races has created a massive psychoexistential complex.[35]

Here Fanon does not say anything about the relations of superordination and subordination that characterize the colonial relationship, a relationship based entirely on color.

Early relations between whites and blacks were not characterized by this inferiority and superiority complex. Gustav Jahoda writes:

> . . . The mere possession of a white skin did not necessarily ensure respect for its owner; for instance, it was not very unusual for Africans to beat up the Governor of a fort who had angered them.[36]

The notions of superordination and subordination and superiority and inferiority developed with the setting up of the colonial regime. With the development of this notion, fostered by the colonial government, all relations between whites and the natives were determined by this. Fanon is, therefore, here talking of the "juxtaposition of the white and the black" within the context of colonial relations.[37] Interpreted in this way, the statement does appear to be consistent with Fanon's earlier statement on the origin of colonial alienation.

Fanon comes close to suggesting that there was no alienation in the pre-colonial society:

> With the exception of a few misfits within the closed environment, we can say that every neurosis, every abnormal manifestation, every affective erethism in an Antillean is the product of his cultural situation.[38]

If we are to take the "cultural situation" as the colonial situation, and the "closed environment" as the close-knit community, characterized by intimate face-to-face relations of the type that anthropologists equate with the pre-colonial society, then Fanon is claiming that alienation is almost unknown in the pre-colonial society. Who then are the "few misfits"? And what gives rise to this condition? It is possible that here the misfits are those suffering from individual alienation, which is different from the collective alienation from which the colonized group suffers. If that is the case, then there should be a distinction between colonial and noncolonial alienation. Fanon does not say anything on this.

We have indicated above that the crux of colonial rule is the relation of superordination and subordination, of one group making another group inferior. It is doubtful that such kinds of relations are unique to the colonial system. History is replete with such examples, and pre-colonial African society is no exception. In the pre-colonial past certain African societies had the caste system, others the feudal system; and the relations of inferiority and superiority between those of the higher caste and those of the lower caste, or between those at the upper end of the feudal order and those at the bottom of it, were not all that different from the relations of superordination and subordination that colonial rule instituted.[39] Kwame Nkrumah, responding to the tendency to paint a romantic picture of African society, writes:

> All available evidence from the history of Africa, up to the eve of the European colonization, shows that African society was neither classless nor devoid of a social hierarchy. Feudalism existed in some parts of Africa before colonization; and feudalism involves a deep and exploitative social stratification. . . .[40]

In the colonial system the criterion for discrimination is the ascriptive one of color. In certain African societies where caste and the feudal system obtained in pre-colonial times, status and differentiation were also based on certain ascriptive criteria of birth or ancestry. The crux of the matter is that in the pre-colonial African society there were instances of differentiation and exploitation based on ascriptive criteria; and if it is the violence, humiliation, and degradation inherent in the colonial regime that give rise to alienation, one cannot conclude that certain pre-colonial African societies were entirely free from this. Fanon could argue that the basic difference between the relations of superordination and subordination in the colonial system and in the pre-colonial African societies is that those who were made inferior in the pre-colonial African societies still remained human beings, whereas colonial rule and the relations it fashioned tried to rob the people under subjugation of their status as human beings. "A feeling of inferiority? No, a feeling of nonexistence."[41] Fanon writes:

> Because it is a systematic negation of the other person and a furious determination to deny the other person all attributes of humanity, colonialism forces the people it dominates to ask themselves the question constantly: "In reality, who am I?"[42]

He claims that in other types of domination this has not been the case: "Under the German occupation the French remained men; under the French occupation, the Germans remained men."[43]

The basic difference between colonial domination and the other forms of domination that Fanon describes does not stand scrutiny. Maquet claims that in Rwanda the Tutsi, who also have relations of superordination and subordination with the Hutu, regard the Hutu as less than human, and they resort to all kinds of theological and cultural arguments to justify their treatment of the Hutu, in the same way the colonialists do with regard to the natives.[44] Admittedly, in the colonial society, color is the basis of the differentiation; in African society, it is birth and ancestry. Although color is easily noticeable, in Rwanda the Tutsi and the Hutu are also easily distinguishable in terms of certain physical features.

Fanon discusses the instruments of colonial alienation. These are physical violence, political oppression, economic deprivation, and social and cultural degradation. These can well operate on the same individual simultaneously. We separate them here only for analytical purposes.

violence

When Fanon writes of violence on the part of the colonizer, he has in mind acts of physical and psychological injury, or force or coercion. On the whole he does not make any distinction between force, violence, power, and coercion. This loose usage of the term *violence* to encompass cases of force, power, and coercion has led to all kinds of varied interpretations of his work.[45]

Fanon argues that violence is an essential part of the colonial situation. It is used at the time of the initiation of colonial rule. Here the various wars of "pacification" and the punitive expeditions with which colonial history is replete are a case in point. Fanon writes:

> The oppressor, in his own sphere, starts the process, a process of domination, of exploitation and of pillage, and in the other sphere the coiled, plundered creature which is the native provides fodder for the process as best he can, the process which moves uninterruptedly from the banks of the colonial territory to the palaces and the docks of the mother country.[46]

There were several instances where colonial rule was initiated by violence; but there were also cases where colonial rule was initiated peacefully by means of treaties, though one has to concede that in a number of treaty-making cases the element of force always lurked in the background. Colonial rule was effected by a mixture of force, violence, persuasion, deceit, and fraud. Whatever element was dominant depended on the particular circumstances of each case.

Fanon claims that not only was the initial settlement of colonial rule achieved through violence and force, but the whole colonial relationship was maintained in the same manner.

> In the colonial countries . . . the policeman and the soldier, by their immediate presence and their frequent and direct action maintain contact with the native and advise him by means of rifle-butts and napalm not to budge. It is obvious here that the agents of government speak the language of pure force.[47]

Contrasting this with the situation in the "mother" countries, Fanon writes:

> In capitalist societies the educational system, whether lay or clerical, the structure of moral reflexes handed down from father to son, the exemplary honesty of workers who are given a medal after fifty years of good and loyal service, and the affection which springs from the harmonious relations and good behavior—all these aesthetic expressions of respect for the established order serve to create around the exploited person an atmosphere of submission and of inhibition which lightens the task of policing considerably. In the capitalist countries a multitude of moral teachers, counselors and "bewilderers" separate the exploited from those in power.[48]

Colonial rule was not maintained by force and violence alone: the colonialists socialized the natives into their value system through the churches and the schools. Although every government relies on some degree of force or threat of force to maintain itself, it is unlikely that colonial rulers could have held the colonies by pure force. Even in areas of permanent European settlements, such as Algeria, Kenya, Angola, Mozambique, Rhodesia, and South Africa, where force and violence were relied upon more than in other areas, it is doubtful that they alone could have maintained power, as Fanon seems to imply in the passage quoted. In fact, Fanon's work *Black Skin, White Masks* describes at length the results of the socialization process that the natives of the colonized countries undergo and the attitudes and behavior patterns that they assume as a result of this. Such reliance on violence and force to the extent to which Fanon describes it is unnecessary to hold down such a group. Furthermore, when we consider the portrait of the native intellectual that Fanon paints, and when we consider that the mass of the population hold the intelligentsia as the reference group, who also hold the colonizers as the reference group, it is not likely that one needs the kind of force and violence described by Fanon to maintain such a group in subjection. Why then does Fanon emphasize so much the aspect of the violence of the colonial regime? Is this the result of his experience in Algeria? In fact, he goes on to claim that it is the oppressor who puts violence into the head of the native:

> The intermediary does not lighten the oppression, nor seek to hide the domination; he shows them up and puts them into practice with the clear conscience of an upholder of the peace; yet he is the bringer of violence into the home and into the mind of the native.[49]

This brings a sharp dissent from Conor Cruise O'Brien, who argues:

> Violence is not, as Fanon often seems to suggest, a creation of colonialism. On the contrary, colonialism is a form of violence: a form developed by the most tightly organized and most effectively violent human societies. The British and the Ashanti, the Belgians and the Bayeke, were alike in that they all wanted power and loot, and used force to get them; the British and the Belgians, disposing of more force, got more power and loot, and the Ashanti and Bayeke became *les colonisés* along with their former subjects, the pre-colonial *colonisés*. As far as violence and power are concerned, colonialism introduced no new principles into Africa, merely the more effective application of existing principles.[50]

O'Brien follows Fanon in his use of the word *violence* interchangeably with *force* or *power*, as the above quotation shows; but that aside, O'Brien seems to have misunderstood Fanon's position. Fanon does not say that violence is a creation of colonialism. He is saying that it is the settler or, specifically, his intermediaries who introduced violence into *the relationship of the native and the settler.*

Fanon is not specific in his discourse on how the violence of the colonial regime causes alienation in the colonized. Presumably, the initial physical violence that accompanies the European presence, or the day-to-day instances of physical violence of the colonial regime, cause a traumatic experience in the native, and this renders his psychic framework out of harmony, thus leading to alienation. It could also be that the physical violence of the colonial regime or the threat of violence produces in the native feelings of fear, humiliation, and inferiority. This statement from Alvin Poussaint, professor of psychiatry at Harvard University, illustrates the point we are trying to make.

> Once last year as I was leaving my office in Jackson, Miss. with my Negro secretary, a white policeman yelled, "Hey boy! Come here." Somewhat bothered I retorted: "I'm no boy." He then rushed at me, inflamed, and stood towering over me, snorting. "What d'ja say, boy?" Quickly he frisked me and demanded, "What's your name boy?" Frightened, I replied, "Dr. Poussaint, I'm a physician." He angrily chuckled and hissed, "What's your first name, boy?" When I hesitated, he assumed a threatening stance and clenched his fists. As my heart palpitated, I muttered in profound humiliation, "Alvin".
>
> He continued . . . "Alvin, the next time I call you, come right away, you hear?" "You hear?" I hesitated, "You hear me, boy?" My voice trembling with helplessness, but following my instincts of self-preservation, I murmured, "Yes, sir."[51]

Such an incident is bound to have a profound psychological impact not only on the individual concerned but on others who happen to be witnesses or on those to whom it is related. It could either raise indignation or produce a deep sense of humiliation and subservience.

Incidents of this nature were not unknown in the colonies. Brecher writes of Nehru in chains being paraded through the streets of New Delhi.[52]

In this way violence is introduced into the relations of the colonizer and the colonized, but due to the fear of severe sanctions or a feeling of inferiority, the violence of the native is repressed.

> This is why the dreams of the native are always of muscular prowess; his dreams are of action and of aggression. I dream I am jumping, swimming, running, climbing; I dream that I burst out laughing, that I span a river in one stride, or that I am followed by a flood of motor-cars which never catch up with me.[53]

O. Mannoni, in his study of the Malagasy, reproduces a number of dreams that bear out Fanon's point, namely, that the dreams deal with action, though Mannoni has a different interpretation of them.[54] The dreams of the colonized are dreams of action, and this is due to the self-repression that the colonial society has forced on the native. During sleep the repressed self assumes its spontaneous nature, hence the dreams of muscular character. If we accept Fanon's interpretation, then we canot avoid the conclusion that as independence is achieved, the muscular action of the dreams will disappear. So far, we are not sure that this has been the case.

Fanon also argues that the dance and ritual of African societies is, in fact, a form of emotional release from the tensions and pressure of the colonial society.

> In the colonial world, the emotional sensitivity of the native is kept on the surface of his skin like an open sore which flinches from the caustic agent; and the psyche shrinks back, obliterates itself and finds outlet in muscular demonstrations which have caused certain very wise men to say that the native is a hysterical type. This sensitive emotionalism, watched by invisible keepers who are, however, in unbroken contact with the core of the personality, will find its fulfilment through eroticism in the driving forces behind the dissolution of the crisis.

> On another level we see the native's emotional sensibility exhausting itself in dances which are more or less ecstatic. . . . The native's relaxation takes precisely the form of a muscular orgy in which the most acute aggressivity and the most impelling violence are canalized, transformed and conjured away.[55]

This interpretation of the dance can only be accepted if we can make a case that in pre-colonial African society the dance in the form of "muscular orgy" was absent, or that the dance was not characterized by intense muscular movements. If we accept Fanon's interpretation, we also cannot avoid the conclusion that with the coming of independence, the dance would lapse. And Fanon, in fact, makes this claim: "During the struggle for freedom, a marked alienation from these practices is observed."[56] We do not have any evidence to support this view. In fact, it is conceivable that the opposite is the case. During the fight for independence, the natives begin to revive all the old traditions and cultures as a way of validating their culture and authenticating their existence. It might even be a strategy for mobilizing the people for the liberation struggle. We have seen the same tendencies in the United States, as blacks begin to revive African dances: the coincidence between this and the intensification of the black struggle for liberation is significant. Besides, if Fanon's argument is accepted, then we should expect the same reactions from American blacks in response to slavery and the oppressive conditions in which they lived; but jazz, which developed specifically out of the conditions in which black people found themselves, is not a type of music that conjures up intense muscular movements.[57] Besides, dances of strong muscular movements are not unique to Africans or even to oppressed people: a number of European folk dances also call for intense muscular movements. It has been claimed that the dance and the rituals associated with them were sometimes employed as a form of resistance to colonial authority.[58]

Fanon would concede that the dance did predate colonial rule, but then he would probably argue that at that time it was a form of entertainment, not the release of muscular tension. But then how is one to know when dance is for entertainment and when it is for the release of muscular tension? During colonial rule one cannot deny that the dance was used as a form of entertainment.

On the question of dreams it should be noted that most societies, African or not, oppressor and oppressed alike, have a folklore in which a great deal of emphasis is put on feats of physical and muscular prowess. In view of this it is not unusual that muscular action should form a part of the collective unconscious of the people, and that this would be shown in their dreams.

Fanon also argues that the native attempts to relieve this repressed violence by visiting it on himself, i.e., on other natives.

> Here we discover the kernel of that hatred of self which is characteristic of racial conflicts in segregated societies. . . .
>
> . . . In reality each man committed suicide when he went for his neighbour.[59]

Sometimes the alienation of the native seeks an outlet in nihilistic acts of self-destruction.

> Thus collective auto-destruction in a very concrete form is one of the ways in which the native's muscular tension is set free.[60]

When the native responds to colonial pressures with such acts as participation in the "muscular orgies" of the dance, violence against the self, acts of collective self-destruction, and the death wish, the colonizer uses them as evidence of the inherent inferiority of the native. Such acts set the native apart. In this way, the colonizer justifies his discriminatory and inhuman treatment of the native. What is, in fact, a response to the oppressive conditions of the native becomes a psychological trait. Fanon reviews the work of two doctors—A. Porot and Carothers[61]—who use this line of reasoning to explain the behavior of the native. The effect of this, according to Fanon, is to give scientific validity to a notion arising out of prejudice. Writing with specific reference to Algeria, he states:

> The Algerian's criminality, his impulsivity and the violence of his murders are therefore not the consequence of the organization of his nervous system nor of a peculiar trait in his character, but the direct product of the colonial situation.[62]

Fanon's contention that colonial rule is violent is a valid one, and one does not need go far to find evidence for it. But colonial rule is not all violence. It is true that violence always lurked in the background. But as Fanon himself shows, the relations were also paternal; and paternal relations are not violent relations, unless one argues that all relations that eventually adversely affect the life and personality of the native are violent relations. We can then talk of psychological violence. But Fanon clearly differentiates the method of rule in the "mother" country from that of the colonies, and argues that in the colonies, colonial rule is maintained by physical violence. To subsume all colonial relations under physical violence is to weaken the analytic utility of the concept. We have to include the notion of psychological violence if Fanon's argument of the pervasiveness of violence in the colonial regime is to stand.

Fanon does not deny the presence of violence in pre-colonial society. If that is the case, how can we be sure that a particular alienation that the native suffers is caused by colonial violence and not pre-colonial violence? Besides, if Fanon argues that only colonial violence causes alienation, what is it about it that does so? His position can only be maintained if it is argued that colonial violence superseded all previous forms of violence.

political oppression

The colonizer controls the political destiny of the colonized, who is not allowed to participate in the political processes that affect him. All decisions that affect him are made by the colonizers, and thus the colonized also suffers political oppression. He is made to feel alien in his own country. Such conditions lead to feelings of humiliation, inferiority, and powerlessness.

It has been argued that the picture that Fanon paints of colonial rule is overdrawn.[63] Olorunsola and Vaitheswaran contend that though Fanon's characterization may approximate in certain ways to the situation in the French or in colon-dominated areas, it did not conform to the reality of what happened in most of Africa. Such arguments claim that due to the institution of indirect rule, the African social and political structures in the former British territories were not destroyed. Hence the colonized did not suffer the excesses of colonial rule sufficiently to feel that profound sense of alienation that Fanon talks of. Fanon maintains that colonial rulers did not destroy African cultures in their entirety, but argues that they were robbed of their essential values and functions:

> The setting up of the colonial system does not of itself bring about the death of the native culture. Historic observation reveals, on the contrary, that the aim sought is rather a continued agony than a total disappearance of the pre-existing culture. This culture, once living and open to the future, becomes closed, fixed in the colonial status, caught in the yoke of oppression. Both present and mummified, it testifies against its members. It defines them in fact without appeal. The cultural mummification leads to a mummification of individual thinking. The apathy so universally noted among colonial peoples is but the logical consequence of this operation.[64]

What Fanon is maintaining is that African culture loses its autonomy and is tagged onto colonial rule so that it becomes one of the instruments of oppression. Anthropologists may dispute Fanon's claim, but there were several cases where the colonial administration kept in office chiefs who had violated all the customary restraints on the office, so long as they remained in the good graces of the colonial administrators. There were customs and traditions that were disallowed because they were offensive to the colonial rulers; others were ridiculed and given low prestige value. In fact, customs that were tolerated or promoted were those that the colonial administrators thought would contribute to the success of their rule or, at least, would not negate it. In this way the culture of the people became an agent of their own oppression. If that is the case, then one could argue that though the naked and brutal aspects of colonial rule varied from area to area depending on the circumstances (whether there was a colon settlement or not) or the strategy of colonial rule (direct or indirect), one has to note that though none of the colonial rulers rigidly followed this pattern, the end result was the same. The African social and political organization was used to serve the ends of the colonial rulers, and in this way the institutions of the people contributed to their own oppression. In such a situation, whether colonial rule was tempered by paternalism or not, the result was the same: alienation.

cultural degradation

Fanon argues that one of the ways by which colonial rule causes alienation of the colonized is through cultural degradation. He discusses in some detail the cultural factors that lead to such alienation. Of these perhaps the most important are education and the language of the colonizer, which remain the most potent instruments for the systematic alienation of the native. In the colonial territory the colonizer first imposes his language on the colonized. The language of the colonizer becomes the official language, the language of commerce and business. The ability to express oneself well in that language grants one automatic entrance to a higher status in the colonial system. In the colonial system the language of the colonizer is not only a medium of communication; it is a "social artifact." Thus, to adopt the language of the colonizer is to assume his cultural forms and thought patterns. Fanon underlines the importance of language:

> I ascribe a basic importance to the phenomenon of language. That is why I find it necessary to begin with this subject, which should provide us with one of the elements in the colored man's comprehension of the dimension of *the other*. For it is implicit that to speak is to exist absolutely for the other.[65]

It is the adoption of the colonizer's language that estranges the native. In the colonial territory the language of the colonizer has a great prestige value. The sentence "he speaks English well" or "he speaks French well" denotes not only a reference to linguistic ability, but also the level of acculturation and acceptance of the white man's ways of life. In Fanon's own words:

> To speak means to be in a position to use a certain syntax, to grasp the morphology of this or that language, but it means above all to assume a culture, to support the weight of a civilization.[66]

Again he writes:

> The Negro . . . will be proportionately whiter—that is, he will come closer to being a real human being—in direct ratio to his mastery of the French language.[67]

In the colony the colonialists are the "real people," hence their language is the "real language." There is a feeling both on the part of the colonizer and on the part of the colonized that the black man or the colonized person comes closer to being a real human being in proportion to his ability to speak the white man's language. As Fanon says, "A man who has a language consequently possesses the world expressed and implied by that language. . . . Mastery of language affords remarkable power."[68] The black man becomes whiter as he renounces his blackness and his culture. It is here that the degradation of the black man's language and culture begins. Fanon writes:

> In the French colonial army, and particularly in the Senegalese regiments, the black officers serve first of all as interpreters. They are used to convey the master's orders to their fellows, and they too enjoy a certain position of honor.[69]

So important was the language of the colonizer regarded that in Martinique the middle classes did not speak Creole to their children; they spoke it only to their servants. In school Martinican children were taught to scorn the dialect, and mothers ridiculed their children for speaking it.[70] Although Fanon is writing here with a specific reference to the Antilles, and although this tendency may exist in exaggerated form there, it is noticeable in varying degrees in all countries that have experienced colonial rule.[71] The expression "he talks like a white man" is not merely a descriptive reference: it is commendatory. In the Antilles so much importance was attached to the language of the white man, that the blacks who returned from France pretended to be no longer able to speak Creole. Fanon claims that every language is a way of thinking, and the fact that the newly returned blacks adopted a language different from that of the group into which they were born is evidence of a dislocation, a separation.[72] But one could argue that if this is so, then everyone who learns a foreign language should expect to be alienated. This, however, is not so. The Frenchman who learns English adopts to some extent the way of thinking of the English when he expresses himself in that language, but the English accept that the Frenchman has a language of his own by means of which important ideas can be expressed. For him, therefore, acceptance of English is not a denial of his own language; it is a tool of communication. In the case of the black man it is not only a question of accepting a language but also one of accepting a culture and a way of thinking to replace his own.

Another aspect of the language question is that whites nearly always talk to blacks in "pidgin," which, in a way, is used not only for the linguistic purpose of facilitating easy communication but as a way of talking down to social inferiors, since they do it routinely to every black, even though he may be proficient in their language. In relating the ridiculous lengths to which the native Martinicans went about the colonizer's language, Fanon relates an incident that occurred on the island in 1945, when Aimé Césaire was campaigning for the seat of deputy in the French National Assembly. During one of the campaign speeches a woman fainted. The following day a friend commented on the incident. Fanon writes:

> In the election campaign of 1945, Aimé Césaire, who was seeking a deputy's seat, addressed a large audience in the boys' school in Fort-de-France. In the middle of his speech a woman fainted. The next day, an acquaintance told me about this and commented: *"Français a te tellement chaud que la femme là tombé malcadi"* (*sic*).[73]

In a footnote he writes, by way of elucidation, "Le français (l'élégance de la forme) était tellement chaud que la femme est tombée en transes."[74]

Furthermore, the system of formal education in the colonial territory was such as to end in the alienation of the native. Here the exercise was to elevate the culture of the colonizer and to denigrate the culture of the colonized. The metropolis and everything connected with it was held in high esteem. The sort of books and stories that children read all tended to promote this. Fanon claims that in every community there is a collective catharsis. The sorts of books that children read in the colonies were designed by white people for white children. This was to enable them to project their aggression on the "other," that is, those defined as outside the group. The evil men, the devils, were and must be members of the out-group, namely, the nonwhite group.[75]

In America the symbols of the bad men are always the Indians or the blacks. These books are specifically meant for white children, to create an opportunity for their catharsis. When children read these books, they naturally identify with the victors or "good guys"; and since the "bad guys" are always those who are perceived to be different from them, these have some psychological value for the white children. For the black children who have access to these materials, the result of this is that they also identify with the victors or "good guys," with whom they do not identify in racial, ethnic, or class terms. The end result of all this is that they tend to hate and despise those who are not of the same ethnic, racial, or class groups as the ones presented to them as ideals, and in this case it is always the blacks or Indians. But then they realize that they are black, or at least nonwhite. Hence, they tend to hate themselves.

Fanon relates how black children in the Antilles talked of "our ancestors, the Gauls."[76] Education was presented in such a way that black children identified with the explorer, the missionary, "the bringer of civilization, the white man who carries truth to the savages—an all-white truth."[77] The effect of this was to make the young black adopt the white man's attitudes and invest the hero, a white person, with all his aggression. In small ways black children came to have a crystallization of attitudes and a way of thinking that was essentially white.[78] Children dreamed of climbing up in the white society, and as they dreamed in this way, they rejected their own social and cultural roots. In addition, white culture was given a high prestige value. As Fanon says, "One is white as one is rich, as one is beautiful, as one is intelligent."[79] Everything white was good, and all good things were related to the white. To be white, therefore, was to be rich, beautiful and intelligent.

In addition to the system of formal education, there were other ways by which the colonial regime tried to ensure the cultural estrangement of the native:

> Colonialism is not satisfied merely with holding a people in its grip and emptying the native's brain of all form and content. By a kind of perverted logic, it turns to the past of the oppressed people, and distorts, disfigures, and destroys it. . . .
>
> When we consider the efforts made to carry out the cultural estrangement so characteristic of the colonial epoch, we realize that nothing has been left to chance and that the total result looked for by colonial domination was indeed to convince the natives that colonialism came to lighten their darkness. The effect consciously sought by colonialism was to drive into the natives' heads the idea that if the settlers were to leave, they would at once fall back into barbarism, degradation, and bestiality.[80]

The church as the moral arm of the colonial state also contributed its share in alienating the native. It helped make him a docile and submissive individual. The values emphasized by the church were those of forgiveness, obedience, humility, and subservience, the qualities necessary for subjection. Fanon says: "All those saints who have turned the other cheek, who have forgiven trespasses against them, and who have been spat on and insulted without shrinking are studied and held up as examples."[81]

Fanon argues that these qualities were often attributed to the whites, and the blacks were enjoined to follow their noble examples. Even though in the relations of whites with blacks these qualities were absent, the church insisted on this fiction to such an extent that the whites appeared in the eyes of the blacks as objects of moral purity; and the blacks saw themselves as the quintessence of evil, and began to develop guilt feelings about themselves.

As if this were not enough, there were other concrete signs that reminded the native of the superior role and status of the colonizer. Here there was the statue of the general who had carried out the conquest; there, the statue of the engineer who had built the bridge.[82]

In addition to the efforts of the colonizer to humiliate and dehumanize the native, the native also assisted in this process by his belief in fatality; this removed all the blame from the oppressor; the cause of his misfortunes and poverty was attributed to God. It was his fate as ordained by God. "In this way," says Fanon, "the individual accepts the disintegration ordained by God, bows down before the settler and his lot, and by a kind of interior restabilization acquires a stony calm."[83] The colonized people, thus oppressed economically, politically, and culturally, begin to think that to exist is to continue to be alive.

> The real people, the men and the women, the children and the old people in the colonized country, take it for granted that existing, in the biological sense of the word, and existing as a sovereign people are synonymous.[84]

In addition, the colonizer tries to dehumanize the native further by creating a stereotype of him and trying to impose this stereotype on him. The colonizer creates the stereotype of the native as a childlike creature; an obsequious, smiling servant. And in the colonies whites adopt the attitude toward the black man that they adopt toward children; they treat him paternally.

Another image that the whites create of the black man is that he is some sort of a "sexual instinct." "For the majority of white men," says Fanon, "the Negro represents the sexual instinct (in its raw state)."[85] The black man is regarded as the incarnation of genital potency beyond all prohibitions. And white women have a tendency to view the black man as the keeper of the impalpable gate that opens into the realm of orgies, of bacchanals, of delirious sexual sensation.[86] Quoting from Michel Cournot's *Martinique*, Fanon writes:

> The black man's sword is a sword. When he has thrust it into your wife, she has really felt something. It is a revelation. In the chasm that it has left, your little toy is lost. Pump away until the room is awash with your sweat, you might as well just be singing. This is *good-by*. . . . Four Negroes with their penises exposed would fill a cathedral. . . .[87]

This kind of sensational writing about the sexual potency of the black man creates in the minds of white people the image of the black man as a personification of sex. Of this passage Frantz Fanon makes the following remark:

> When one reads this passage a dozen times and lets oneself go —that is, when one abandons oneself to the movement of its images—one is no longer aware of the Negro but only of a penis; the Negro is eclipsed. He is turned into a penis. He *is* a penis.[88]

In addition to the sexual image of the black that the white society builds, the black man is also painted as a symbol of evil. As Fanon puts it, "Both of us stand for Evil. The black man more so, for the good reason that he is black. Is not whiteness in symbols always ascribed in French to Justice, Truth, Virginity?"[89] Commenting on the inferiority with which the black man is encased, he says:

> A feeling of inferiority? No, a feeling of nonexistence. Sin is Negro as virtue is white. All those white men in a group, guns in their hands, cannot be wrong. I am guilty. I do not know of what, but I know that I am no good.[90]

Here, the black man begins to develop guilt feelings that he is evil, that he is inferior, that, after all, the white man is right. There must be something wrong with him, something he does not know quite clearly, but he at least knows that there is something evil about him.

The black man is not treated simply as a man. He is treated as a black man, that is, in reference to the stereotypes that the white man has created of him. He is expected to respond and act according to these stereotypes.

> A man was expected to behave like a man. I was expected to behave like a black man—or at least like a nigger.[91]

The tragedy of all this is that the black man also assumes the characteristics and the stereotypes that the white man has created. Fanon writes:

> The inferiorized group had admitted, since the force of reasoning was implacable, that its misfortunes resulted directly from its racial and cultural characteristics.
>
> Guilt and inferiority are the usual consequences of this dialectic. The oppressed then tries to escape these, on the one hand by proclaiming his total and unconditional adoption of the new cultural models, and on the other, by pronouncing an irreversible condemnation of his own cultural style.[92]

Fanon compares the position of the blacks with that of the Jews. The Jew, he says, is a slave of the "idea" that others have of him, but the black man is a slave of his own appearance.[93] Hence, whereas the Jew can escape, the black man cannot. Fanon thinks that even liberal whites are not very different in the way they conceive of the black man. They concede, at least, that the black man is a human being, that he is a human being in the biological sense of the word, but that is all.

> . . . Like us he has his heart on the left side. But on certain points the white man remained intractable. Under no conditions did he wish any intimacy between the races, for it is a truism that "crossings between widely different races can lower the physical and mental level. . . ."[94]

Racism and racial segregation have also been used by the colonizers to dehumanize the colonized. In nearly all colonial territories racial discrimination has been an official policy. Even in Senegal, where assimilation was put into practice in a more determined way than in any other colony, it must be noted that the assimilationist policy was permitted only in the Four Communes, and even here there were flagrant departures from the proclaimed policy.[95] Elsewhere, it was the policy of association that was based on racist foundations. In all areas of colonial rule there is strict segregation on the basis of race. There is always the European part of the city, with all its amenities, and the native part of the city. There is also the European school, the European hospital, and the European church. Even in territories where no legal segregation exists, racial segregation is socially enforced; and whites and blacks do not enjoy the same conditions of service and privileges, even if they are both equally qualified and holding the same rank. Rarely is any African, no matter how well qualified, put into a position where he will have to give instructions to whites.[96]

It must be conceded that in the early period of European contact with the west coast of Africa, not much attention was paid to the racial factor, but when the relationship changed from that of traders to that of the colonizer and the colonized, race became a crucial factor in all the relations between whites and blacks.

Fanon regards racism as one of the instruments of cultural degradation. In response to the argument of Mannoni that racism has nothing to do with economic factors, Fanon points out that in South Africa the displacement of the white proletariat's aggression onto the black proletariat is fundamentally a result of the economic structure.[97] He also discounts the argument of Mannoni that racism is the work of petty officials, and contends that South Africa is racist because it has a racist structure. What he means is that racism was fundamentally economic in South Africa, but as time went on it became part of the social structure and acquired an almost independent existence. It is in this sense that one can say that a society has a racist structure.

Initially, racism employed crude biological arguments to justify its position. This was the period of "crude racism" and corresponded in Fanon's view to the period of crude exploitation. Later, it was to assume a more subtle form, "cultural racism." This corresponds with the current period of racism. It is held that the black man is on a low evolutionary plane and that, in order to achieve equality, he has to approximate to the cultural level of the white man. In theory the basis of differentiation is the difference in cultural level and style of life. In order to reach the human level, the native tries to deracialize himself. The "inferior" race, then, denies itself as a different race. It shares with the "superior race" the convictions, doctrines, and other attitudes concerning it.[98] What follows is the liquidation of the natives' systems of reference and the collapse of their cultural patterns. The colonizer imposes on the colonized his own framework of judging the native and a pejorative judgment with respect to the colonized's original form of existing.[99] Guilt and an inferiority complex are the results of this process. The oppressed try to escape their inferiority by proclaiming on the one hand the total acceptance of the cultural models of the colonizer and, on the other hand, the condemnation of his own cultural style.[100] The oppressed then abandons his language and his cultural habits, and he accepts the cultural imposition of the colonizer. But he finds that all this is to no avail. He is still regarded as different and inferior. Fanon writes:

> Having judged, condemned, abandoned his cultural forms, his language, his food habits, his sexual behavior, his way of sitting down, of resting, of laughing, of enjoying himself, the oppressed *flings himself* upon the imposed culture with the desperation of a drowning man.
>
> Developing his technical knowledge in contact with more and more perfected machines, entering into the dynamic circuit of industrial production, meeting men from remote regions in the framework of the concentration of capital, that is to say, on the job, discovering the assembly line, the team, production "time," in other words yield per hour, the oppressed is shocked to find that he continues to be the object of racism and contempt.[101]

The native finds that he is trapped, that whatever he does, the racist imposition on his humanity and his culture will not cease. Racism is a necessary counterpart of colonial rule.

> It is not possible to enslave men without logically making them inferior through and through. And racism is only the emotional, affective, sometimes intellectual explanation of this inferiorization.[102]

Again Fanon writes:

> Race prejudice in fact obeys a flawless logic. A country that lives, draws its substance from the exploitation of other peoples, makes those peoples inferior. Race prejudice applied to those peoples is normal.[103]

The position that Fanon wishes to emphasize is that racism is the consequence and not the cause of the system of exploitation of one group of people by another group. Appeals to the human spirit, therefore, that do not fundamentally alter the situation of exploitation are futile.

economic deprivation

Unlike Marx, Fanon does not talk of economic alienation. Marx's concept of economic alienation in the sense of the loss of the control of the producer over his produce, or of monotonous working conditions, does not figure at all in any of Fanon's discussions on alienation. However, when we consider the role of the urban worker in the colonies, or the farmer who has to produce cash crops in response to the demands of the colonial government, the relations of the worker with his produce are not that much different from what Marx depicted. After all, we also have to remember that colonial society is a capitalist society, though in a peripheral relationship to the metropolitan capitalist society, and the specialization of labor that results in alienation is also present in the colonial society, though not to the same extent as in the advanced capitalist or socialist countries. Fanon, probably because of his training, was led to emphasize the psychological and cultural aspects of alienation, to the neglect of the economic aspects.

The blatant violence of colonial rule, the political and economic oppression, the cultural dehumanization, the attitude of treating the colonized as if they are "things," all contribute to alienating the black man from himself, from his other fellow blacks, and from his culture.

ways in which alienation is expressed

One of the ways in which the alienation of the colonized is expressed is through the manifestation of a feeling of inferiority. Because of this feeling of inferiority, the colonized try to compensate for this by trying to imitate the colonizer. The colonized community also behaves with unusual reverence toward those members of the colonized group who have had some intimate contact with the colonizer. Fanon indicates that, in Martinique, the mere prospect of going to Europe caused changes in the behavior and outlook of the black man.

> There is a kind of magic vault of distance, and the man who is leaving next week for France creates round himself a magic circle in which the words *Paris*, *Marseille*, *Sorbonne*, *Pigalle* become the keys to the vault. He leaves for the pier, and the amputation of his being diminishes as the silhouette of his ship grows clearer. In the eyes of those who have come to see him off he can read the evidence of his own mutation, his power. "Good-by bandanna, good-by straw hat. . . ."[104]

Those who are returning from the metropolis also exhibit the same characteristics. In Fanon's words:

> The "newcomer" reveals himself at once; he answers only in French, and often he no longer understands Creole.[105]
>
> He no longer understands the dialect, he talks about the Opéra, which he may never have seen except from a distance, but above all he adopts a critical attitude toward his compatriots.[106]

This idea of trying to approximate to the colonizer is not only to be found in the relations of the black man with the white man. It is to be noted that the black man sometimes tries to approximate his status to the status of other blacks if he thinks that they enjoy a higher status or are culturally near the white man. Fanon tells us of the case of some Congolese who try to pass as natives of the Antilles. Antilleans get offended when they are mistaken for Senegalese. This is because the Antillean is supposed to be more civilized and consequently has a higher status than the Senegalese.[107] Not long ago, black Americans were offended when mistaken for Africans, because at that time the black American was made to feel that he was more civilized than the African.[108]

Another consequence that the blacks suffer as a result

of this oppression and dehumanization is a form of self-hatred. They dislike other black people, which is a form of dislike of oneself. They express some of the most racist stereotypes about the black man. Fanon writes, "In the man of color there is a constant effort to run away from his own individuality, to annihilate his own presence."[109] He also relates, as noted earlier, the case of a black girl living in Paris who kept a list of dance halls where she was sure of not running into blacks.[110] There were also a number of black women who admitted to him that they would never marry black men. One told him in anger:

> If Césaire makes so much display about accepting his race, it is because he really feels it is a curse. . . . As far as I am concerned, I wouldn't marry a Negro for anything in the world.[111]

Fanon adds that such attitudes were not rare.

Colonial alienation has also conditioned the native to seek his being in the white man. This is manifested by a tendency to attract the attention of the colonizer and to seek recognition from him. Colonial alienation is also expressed by a feeling of inadequacy and a sense of dependency.[112] Fanon does not deny the characteristics with which the whites of the colonial society endow the native, but argues that they are caused by the colonial society, and not the inherent characteristics of the colonized.

Fanon shows that the phenomenon of alienation that occurs in the colonial society also occurs after the country has achieved independence.[113] The national bourgeoisie of the former dependent countries manifest all the outward signs of alienation: a feeling of inferiority, a feeling of inadequacy, a feeling of other-directedness with regard to the former colonizers and white people in general.

The reason for this is that there has not been a change

of consciousness. The alienated native has not overcome his alienated consciousness, which in Fanon's view can be achieved through revolutionary violence. The way by which most of the African countries gained independence was such that it did not lead to a change of consciousness. In the absence of a revolution the elites just assumed control of the social, political, and economic institutions of the colonized society. This transfer of authority, which is called independence, Fanon regards as localization of colonial rule, since the institutions have not changed nor have the relations between the ruler and the ruled.[114] In such conditions the phenomenon of alienation persists.

Alienation is one of the most important themes in Fanon's thought, and he devotes a lot of space to discussing it. In fact, the whole of *Black Skin, White Masks* is a study in alienation. His treatment of the subject, however, raises a number of questions, some of which we have dealt with in the preceding pages.

Fanon does not define the term *alienation*. He sometimes uses different words or phrases to identify the same phenomenon. He also uses *alienation* and *neurosis* interchangably. In spite of this, it is clear that when he uses the term *alienation*, or writes of the phenomenon, he has in mind some kind of separation of the person from his individuality, or from his existential condition, or from his culture or community, or from his essential self.

Fanon also assumes that alienation implies separation where unity once prevailed, and he tends to think that this unity prevailed in the pre-colonial society. As we have demonstrated above, his image of the pre-colonial society is too general and does not bear any relation to reality. Besides, from what we know of the relations between individuals or groups in societies like Rwanda, it is extremely unlikely that alienation did not exist.

Fanon talks of violence as playing a very important part in colonial alienation. He does not define the term, and he uses it in a sense that embodies the connotations we associate with force, power, coercion, and the like. Such loose usage of such a critical term weakens its analytic utility. Another important weakness in Fanon's discussion on violence and alienation is that he does not say in what precise manner violence causes the alienation of the native. We know, for instance, that in the colonized society the violence of the colonizer was not the only form of violence, and that the colonized was also violent. How can we be sure that a particular alienation expressed by a particular person is not the result of the natives' own violence, different from the violence of the colonial regime? The only way Fanon can maintain his position is to assume that there was no violence in African society prior to the institution of colonial rule. Alternatively, he could argue that the violence of the colonial regime superseded all other forms of violence of the native. And this is the position Fanon takes. But the question is: What is it about colonial violence that makes it supersede all the other forms of violence of the native? Is it the intensity or the scale? He overcomes the problem by defining colonial rule as violence. This, as we have already indicated, makes sense only when we take colonial violence in its totality—structural, psychological, social, and physical. Fanon, however, in one instance of differentiating between the method of rule employed in the metropolis and that employed in the colonies insists on physical violence as the defining characteristic of colonial rule. And this, as we have had occasion to point out above, not only is inadequate but is also contradicted by the evidence of his *Black Skin, White Masks*. Furthermore, Fanon's attempt to explain the effect of colonial violence on the native by recourse to the Freudian concept of compensation is inadequate. African dances cannot be explained simply in terms of overcoming violence through the release of muscular tension.

Fanon's discussion on alienation is always couched

in the negative, that is, it is what it ought not to be. He does not give us any picture of the non-alienated man against which we can measure the question of alienation. What is the free, autonomous, non-alienated individual? How do we know when we have achieved this status?[115]

Fanon sometimes gives the impression that the colonized man is completely determined. If that is the situation, then de-alienation becomes an impossibility. If one is completely alienated, how can one achieve the consciousness of resistance and de-alienation? Sometimes Fanon makes it clear that alienation is not complete: "He is treated as an inferior but he is not convinced of his inferiority."[116] The second usage is consistent with Fanon's argument, for it is only in such a situation that the question of overcoming of alienation will be possible.

Despite the lack of conceptual clarity of the term *alienation* and the numerous problems connected with Fanon's discourse on the phenomenon, alienation is a useful concept in a discussion of the relations between the black man and the white man. It explains the totality of the black man's existence in a white-dominated world. In view of this, some of the manifestations we associate with alienation in colonial society are also noticeable among black people in the United States, though their condition may not be exactly similar to colonial relationships. The crux of the matter is that they live in a white-dominated society. Fanon's interest in alienation does not end with an analysis of the phenomenon. He is also concerned with ways of overcoming alienation. This brings us to his discussion on revolutionary violence, which is the subject of the next chapter.

1. It could, of course, also be that the term is enjoying some reputation; hence, the popularity of the writers.

2. Of these, the best-known works are: Richard Schacht, *Alienation* (Garden City, N.Y.: Doubleday, 1971); Bertell Ollman, *Alienation: Marx's Conception of Man in Capitalist Society* (Cambridge: At the University Press, 1971); István Mészáros, *Marx's Theory of Alienation* (London: Merlin Press, 1970); Arnold S. Kaufman, "On Alienation," *Inquiry* 8 (Summer 1965): 141-65; Lewis Feuer, "What Is Alienation? The Career of a Concept," *New Politics* 1 (Spring 1962): 116-34; Irving Louis Horowitz, "On Alienation and the Social Order," *Philosophy and Phenomenological Research* 27 (December 1966): 230-37; and Martin Bronfenbrenner, "A Harder Look at Alienation," *Ethics* 83 (July 1973): 267-82.

3. *Black Skin, White Masks*, p. 31. The original French version reads: "Nous répondrons à ces objecteurs que nous faisons ici le procès des mystifiés et des mystificateurs, des aliénés . . . " (*Peau noire, masques blancs*, p. 45).

4. *Black Skin, White Masks*, p. 29. The French version reads: "Je parle ici, d'une part, de Noirs aliénés (mystifiés), et d'autre part de Blancs non moins aliénés (mystificateurs et mystifiés)" (*Peau noire, masques blancs*, p. 43).

5. *Black Skin, White Masks*, p. 14.

6. Ibid., p. 38.

7. Ibid., p. 60.

8. Ibid.

9. Ibid., p. 225.

10. Ibid., p. 204.

11. Ibid.

12. Ibid., p. 208.

13. Ibid., p. 209.

14. Ibid., p. 48.

15. Ibid., p. 224.

16. Ibid.

17. Ibid., p. 10.

18. *Toward the African Revolution*, p. 38.

19. Most of these are sociologists; see Robert Bluner, *Alienation and Freedom* (Chicago: University of Chicago Press, 1964).

20. In particular, Hegel; see *The Phenomenology of Mind.*

21. *Black Skin, White Masks*, p. 13.

22. Ibid., p. 14.

23. Ibid.

24. This is discussed in the next chapter.

25. Albert Memmi, *The Colonizer and the Colonized* (Boston: Beacon Press, 1967).

26. *The Wretched of the Earth*, p. 143.

27. *Black Skin, White Masks*, p. 16.

28. Fanon, *The Wretched of the Earth*, pp. 90-91.

29. Fanon, *Black Skin, White Masks*, p. 10.

30. Not all relations of superordination and subordination are alienation-producing. Here we are talking of a situation where the human status of the subordinate person is denied by his superior.

31. Fanon, *Black Skin, White Masks*, p. 11.

32. Ibid., p. 35.

33. Ibid., p. 17.

34. Ibid., p. 13.

35. Ibid., p. 14.

36. Gustav Jahoda, *White Man* (London: Oxford University Press, 1961), p. 2. See also K. Onwuka Dike, *Trade and Politics in the Niger Delta, 1830–1885* (Oxford: Clarendon Press, 1956), pp. 9, 16–17.

37. These relations have become so much a part of the behavior patterns of the colonizer and the colonized that, in spite of the formal withdrawal of the colonial authority, relations still, to a large extent, are determined by these notions.

38. *Black Skin, White Masks*, p. 152.

39. Jacques Maquet describes such a relationship between the Tutsi and the Hutu of Rwanda; see *The Premise of Inequality in Ruanda* (London: Oxford University Press, 1961).

40. Kwame Nkrumah, "African Socialism Revisited," *African Forum* 1 (Winter 1966): 5.

41. Fanon, *Black Skin, White Masks*, p. 139.

42. *The Wretched of the Earth*, p. 200.

43. Ibid., p. 201.

44. *The Premise of Inequality in Ruanda.*

45. This is treated fully in the next chapter.

46. *The Wretched of the Earth*, p. 39.

47. Ibid., p. 29.

48. Ibid.

49. Ibid.

50. Conor Cruise O'Brien, "The Neurosis of Colonialism," *Nation* 200 (June 1965): 674.

51. Alvin Poussaint, "A Negro Psychiatrist Explains the Negro Psyche," in Norman Yetman and C. Hoy Steele, eds., *Majority and Minority* (Boston: Allyn and Bacon, 1971), p. 346. African writers have from time to time depicted the physical violence that underlies colonial rule: see Ferdinand Oyono, *The Old Man and the Medal* (New York: Collier Books, 1971); translated from the French by John Reed.

52. Michael Brecher, *Nehru: A Political Biography* (London: Oxford University Press, 1959), p. 90.

53. Fanon, *The Wretched of the Earth*, p. 40.

54. O. Mannoni, *Prospero and Caliban: The Psychology of Colonization*, 2d ed. (New York: Praeger, 1964), pp. 89-93.

55. *The Wretched of the Earth*, p. 44.

56. Ibid., p. 45.

57. For information on black dance in the United States, see Lynne Fauley Emery, *Black Dance* (Palo Alto, Calif.: National Press, 1972).

58. Norman Klein, "On Revolutionary Violence," *Studies on the Left* 4 (May-June 1966): 62-82; see also Clyde Mitchell, *The Kalela Dance* (Manchester, England: Manchester University Press, 1967).

59. *The Wretched of the Earth*, p. 250.

60. Ibid., p. 42.

61. Fanon probably had in mind J. C. Carothers, *The African Mind in Health and Disease: A Study in Ethnopsychiatry* (Geneva: W.H.O. Monograph Series, No. 17, 1953).

62. *The Wretched of the Earth*, p. 250.

63. Victor Olorunsola and Ramakris Vaitheswaran, "Reflections Prompted by Frantz Fanon's *The Wretched of the Earth*," *Journal of Developing Areas* 5 (October 1971): 124.

64. *Toward the African Revolution*, p. 34.

65. *Black Skin, White Masks*, p. 17.

66. Ibid., pp. 17-18.

67. Ibid., p. 18.

68. Ibid.

69. Ibid., pp. 18-19.

70. Ibid., p. 20.

71. Ibid. It is important here to recall Léopold Senghor's ecstatic appreciation of the French language: "I am not claiming that French is superior to these other languages, neither in beauty or richness [sic], but I do say that it is the supreme language for *communication*: 'a language of politeness and honesty,' a language of beauty and clarity" (L. Senghor, "Negritude and the Concept of Universal Civilization," *Présence Africaine* 18 (Second Quarter, 1963): 10).

72. Fanon, *Black Skin, White Masks*, p. 25.

73. Ibid., p. 39.

74. Ibid.

75. We may concede that black as a symbol of evil was conceived by Europeans long before their contact with black people. With the emergence of racist ideologies in the nineteenth century, such symbols took on added significance.

76. Ibid., p. 147.

77. Ibid.

78. Ibid., p. 148. Eldridge Cleaver writes of how he idealized a white "pin-up girl" (see *Soul on Ice* [New York: Dell Publishing, Delta Books, 1968], pp. 7-8).

79. *Black Skin, White Masks*, pp. 51-52.

80. Fanon, *The Wretched of the Earth*, p. 169.

81. Ibid., p. 52. It is quite conceivable that the missionaries did not consciously attempt to produce subservient subjects for the colonial administration. They would have probably preached the same values in their own countries; but to preach submission and humility as values to people under domination is to make them accept their status.

82. Ibid., p. 40.

83. Ibid., p. 42.

84. Fanon, *Toward the African Revolution*, p. 78.

85. *Black Skin, White Masks*, p. 177.

86. Ibid.

87. Ibid., p. 169.

88. Ibid., pp. 169-70.

89. Ibid., p. 180. The "both" refers to the black and the Jew. The Jew is also regarded as evil, Fanon says.

90. Ibid., p. 139.

91. Ibid., p. 114.

92. *Toward the African Revolution*, pp. 38-39. For evidence of black assumption of the stereotypes that whites impose on them, see Gustav Jahoda, *White Man*.

93. *Black Skin, White Masks*, p. 116.

94. Ibid., p. 120.

95. For a detailed study of French assimilation policy in Africa, see: Michael Crowder, *Senegal: A Study in French Assimilation Policy* (London: Oxford University Press, 1962); Ruth S. Morgenthau, *Political Parties in French-Speaking West Africa* (Oxford: Clarendon Press, 1964); Martin Deming Lewis, "One Hundred Million Frenchmen: The 'Assimilation' Theory in French Colonial Policy," *Comparative Studies in Society and History* 4 (January 1962).

96. See the career of Africanus Horton (Christopher Fyfe, *Africanus Horton* [New York: Oxford University Press, 1972]).

97. *Black Skin, White Masks*, p. 87. Other black writers have argued in similar terms; see Eric Williams, *Capitalism and Slavery* (New York: Capricorn, 1966).

98. Fanon, *Toward the African Revolution*, p. 38.

99. Ibid.

100. Ibid., pp. 38-39.

101. Ibid., p. 39.

102. Ibid., p. 40.

103. Ibid., pp. 40-41.

104. Fanon, *Black Skin, White Masks*, p. 23.

105. Ibid.

106. Ibid., p. 24.

107. Ibid., pp. 25-26.

108. Coleman, *Nigeria*, pp. 233, 461 n. 8.

109. *Black Skin, White Masks*, p. 60.

110. Ibid., p. 50.

111. Ibid., p. 48.

112. For a detailed description of such aspects of black behavior, see Franklin Frazier, *Black Bourgeoisie*, and Nathan Hare, *The Black Anglo-Saxons*. It should be noted that blacks in America have the same relations with the white society, hence they manifest the same phenomena.

113. See *The Wretched of the Earth*.

114. Jitendra Mohan uses this theme to explain politics in Ghana under the Nkrumah regime; see "Nkrumah and Nkrumaism," *Socialist Register*, 1967, pp. 191-228.

115. Unlike Fanon, Trotsky presents a picture of the non-alienated, fully emancipated man; see *Literature and Revolution* (New York: International Publishers, 1925), p. 256.

116. *The Wretched of the Earth*, p. 41.

chapter five

paths to freedom: revolutionary violence

Violence alone, violence committed by the people, violence organized and educated by its leaders, makes it possible for the masses to understand social truths and gives the key to them. Without that struggle, without that knowledge of the practice of action, there's nothing but a fancy-dress parade and the blare of the trumpets. There's nothing save a minimum of readaptation, a few reforms at the top, a flag waving: and down there at the bottom an undivided mass, still living in the Middle Ages, endlessly marking time.

Frantz Fanon, *The Wretched of the Earth*

We have seen that alienation is the most serious obstacle to the liberation of the colonized person. The task now is how to overcome it. This brings Fanon to the question of revolutionary violence. Fanon argues that it is only by violence that the colonized can achieve their freedom. Violence first liberates consciousness, and second, it destroys the social and political institutions of the colonial society. It is necessary to destroy these institutions because they were set up not for free individuals but as instruments of oppression. Breaking the colonial social, economic, and political structure is the first precondition for freedom of the colonized. The task of this chapter is to discuss Fanon's argument for the necessity of revolutionary violence for the liberation of the colonized.

violence and revolution

Two critical concepts associated with Fanon's argument for freedom are violence and revolution. Since they play a central role in his discussion on the subject, it is necessary to get conceptual clarification of these two terms before we proceed to examine his argument.

There is now a copious literature on violence and revolution, and there is no need to review it here.[1] We shall therefore confine ourselves to the use of these terms in the works of Fanon.

Although Fanon employs the word *violence* quite often in his works, especially in *The Wretched of the Earth*, he nowhere defines it. A close examination, however, shows that he uses it in several senses. He uses it, for instance, to indicate a purposeful act of physical injury. This is one sense in which he talks about the colonial regime as being created and maintained by violence.

> Their first encounter was marked by violence and their existence together—that is to say the exploitation of the native by the settler—was carried on by dint of a great array of bayonets and cannon.[2]

Though Fanon defines the colonial regime in terms of violence, he speaks at the same time of force. "It is obvious here that the agents of government speak the language of pure force."[3] In fact, he uses the terms *violence* and *force* interchangeably. He writes:

. . . The hecatombs are an indication that between oppressors and oppressed everything can be solved by force.[4]

Again:

We have seen that it is the intuition of the colonized masses that their liberation must, and can only, be achieved by force.[5]

Sometimes Fanon uses the adjective *violent* to mean radical or militant:

We may in the same way come to understand the new tone which swamped international diplomacy at the United Nations General Assembly in September 1960. The representatives of the colonial countries were aggressive and violent, and carried things to extremes. . . . The radicalism of the African spokesmen brought the abscess to a head and showed up the inadmissible nature of the veto and of the dialogue between the great powers, and above all the tiny role reserved for the Third World.[6]

To complicate matters further, Fanon talks of "peaceful violence."[7] This refers to the state of international tension or the cold war, the state of "no war, no peace" that existed in the early sixties. It is a state of potential violence. This ambiguity has prompted one critic to write:

But I ask all those who are readers of Fanon to make an experiment: Every time you find the word "violence" in his pages, substitute for it the phrase "radical and uncompromising action." I contend that with the exception of a very few passages this substitution can be made, and that the action he calls for could as well be nonviolent action.[8]

This contention cannot be sustained. It is true that Fanon's usage is not clear, but in most cases when he uses the term *violence* he has in mind anything but nonviolence. To regard Fanon's advocacy of violence and especially *The Wretched of the Earth* as a plea for nonviolence, as Barbara Deming does, is the most bizarre interpretation we have of Fanon. The conceptual ambiguity of the term has also led one writer complain:

> In fact, Fanon's reliance on the notion of violence prevents its clearer definition as a dynamic within decolonization: violence, used to explain everything, explains nothing.[9]

Zolberg, in the same vein, has written: "It would thus seem that 'violence' encompasses almost the entire range of political pressure."[10] One can accuse Fanon of confusing violence with force. What has to be realized is that our own usual employment of the term is frought with ambiguities. Violence does involve, though not always, some force. Force may also, but not always, involve violence; it is possible to apply force without recourse to violence. We sometimes also use the word *violence* in senses that imply neither force nor violence, as when we say, "The violence of his language set the crowd surging forward." Here all we mean is that he used inflammatory language. To complicate matters, for most people *violence* is not a neutral word but has a strong emotive connotation of condemnable action. Considering such ambiguities in our own usage of the term, is it surprising that we find these in Fanon? In the way in which Fanon uses the term it encompasses physical or psychological injury, aggression, militancy or radicalism, coercion, power, or force. One way to overcome the ambiguity and to make some sense out of Fanon is to determine in each context what exactly he means by the term, taking into consideration all the connotations we have given above. If the term *violence* is frought with ambiguities and defies definition, *revolution* is by no means different, as anyone who has taken but a casual look at the literature will no doubt recognise. Karl Kautsky has made this point very well: "There are a few concepts over which there has been so much contention as that of revolution. . . . Few things are so ambiguous."[11] We have to be careful, therefore, when discussing this concept in Fanon. In fact, Fanon makes sparing use of the term *revolution*. He uses other terms to denote the idea of revolution or different dimensions of it; his favorites are *liberation*, *independence*, and *decolonization*.[12] By *independence* Fanon generally refers to the freeing of a colonial territory from external control. This implies revolution in the political sense of the word or the political dimension of the concept.[13] By *decolonization* he means the concept of freeing a territory from external control, together with the destruction of the social and political institutions of the former colonial power and the building of new institutions and relationships to reflect the reality of the nation. It is a fundamental change in the consciousness of the people of the country. What Fanon calls decolonization, Herbert Marcuse calls revolution,

> the overthrow of a legally established government and constitution by a social class or movement with the aim of altering the social as well as the political structure.[14]

Fanon, however, goes much further. For him revolution also implies a sudden, and violent, change. We have to admit that, although Marcuse concedes that such radical and qualitative changes as he has in mind imply violence, unlike Fanon he does not actually build it into his definition.[15] For Fanon the insistence on violence is absolute and unequivocal. "Decolonization [i.e., revolution] is always a violent phenomenon."[16] For Fanon decolonization implies not only a fundamental change in the political, social, cultural, and economic structure of society but also a change of consciousness. It constitutes a change in the individual's perception of reality and world view. Indeed, it is a psychic change, a change of man's entire being. In Fanon's own words:

> . . . Decolonization is quite simply the replacing of a certain "species" of men by another "species" of men. Without any period of transition, there is a total, complete and absolute substitution.[17]

Here the change involves the change of men as well as institutions. It is the creation of a new species of men, not men of a different color or a different social class, but men with a different consciousness, in short, with non-alienated consciousness. Stressing the same theme Fanon writes:

> Decolonization . . . influences individuals and modifies them fundamentally. . . . It brings a natural rhythm into existence, introduced by new men, and with it a new language and a new humanity. Decolonization is the veritable creation of new men. But this creation owes nothing of its legitimacy to any supernatural power; the "thing" which has been colonized becomes man during the same process by which it frees itself.[18]

Decolonization also means a change of "the whole social structure from the bottom to the top." Stressing the fundamental nature of this change, Fanon writes:

> "The last shall be the first and the first last." Decolonization is the putting into practice of this sentence.[19]

And concerning the violence that inevitably accompanies decolonization, Fanon writes:

> For if the last shall be first, this will only come to pass after a murderous and decisive struggle between the two protagonists. That affirmed intention to place the last at the head of things, and to make them climb . . . the well-known steps . . . can only triumph if we use all means to turn the scale, including, of course, that of violence.[20]

For Fanon, therefore, decolonization is a violent revolution that not only destroys the social and political structures of the colonial regime but also liberates consciousness and creates new men.

Why does Fanon argue that it is only through revolutionary violence that the colonized can be liberated? Here we have to remember that for him freedom implies the liberation of consciousness as well as a fundamental change in the socioeconomic environment. Revolutionary violence frees man's consciousness, creates a new man, and at the same time destroys the social and political institutions that act as the mechanisms of his oppression and enslavement, and builds new institutions that allow man to maintain and express his freedom.

violence as a liberating force

Fanon argues that violence is a cleansing force. It frees the colonized from his feeling of inferiority and humiliation and restores him to the fullness of himself as a man.[21] Such importance does Fanon attach to this emancipatory role of violence that he reproduces a passage from Aimé Césaire's *Et les chiens se taisaient*, which exemplifies this position, in both *Black Skin, White Masks* and *The Wretched of the Earth*.

> We broke down the doors. The master's room was wide open. The master's room was brilliantly lighted, and the master was there, quite calm . . . and we stopped. . . . He was the master. . . . I entered. "It is you," he said to me, quite calmly. . . . It was I. It was indeed I, I told him, the good slave, the faithful slave, the slavish slave, and suddenly his eyes were two frightened cockroaches on a rainy day. . . . *I struck, the blood flowed: that is the only baptism that I remember today.*[22] (Emphasis added.)

We can understand this use of violence if we remember that baptism is the symbolic termination of the individual's past life and the beginning of a new one. In the same way, Fanon sees violence as performing the function of marking the termination of the individual's previous life as a "thing" and the beginning of his new life as a human being. This rebirth of the individual[23] has also a direct bearing on the nature of the political system after decolonization. The individual who has gained consciousness of himself as a liberated individual, in the same way that he will no longer submit himself to the tyranny of the colonial oppressor, will also not submit himself to native tyrants but will hold his leaders accountable for their actions. Hence democracy will ensue.

> When the people have taken violent part in the national liberation they will allow no one to set themselves up as "liberators." They show themselves to be jealous of the results of their action and take good care not to place their future, their destiny or the fate of their country in the hands of a living god.[24]

Fanon is not alone in this humanistic appeal to violence as a liberating force for man. Sorel, who regarded the existing capitalist society as corrupt and beyond redemption, also argued for the total destruction of society and the creation of a new man. This was to be accomplished through violence, and the agents of the use of violence were to be the urban working class. Just as Fanon regards the peasants as pure, Sorel regards the proletariat as the only pure and non-corrupted class. Sorel argues in the same way as Fanon would that his violence must be distinguished from conventional violence, not necessarily in its practical effect, but in its essence. His violence was pure violence. There was nothing sadistic or vindictive about it. It did not stem from hatred, but from the humanistic notion of the emancipation of man. Jean-Paul Sartre also shares the view of the emancipatory role of violence. In *Iron in the Soul* he writes: "He fired. He was cleansed. He was all powerful. He was free."[25] In the same way Richard Wright in *Native Son* makes Bigger Thomas a "man" after he has killed Mary Dalton.

> And, yet, out of it all, over and above all that had happened, impalpable but real, there remained to him a queer sense of power. *He* had done this. *He* had brought all this about. In all of his life these two murders were the most meaningful things that had ever happened to him. He was living, truly and deeply, no matter what others might think, looking at him with their blind eyes. Never had he had the chance to live out the consequences of his actions; never had his will been so free as in this night and day of fear and murder and flight.[26]

Before, Bigger was a "thing," an object on which others acted; now he is a man, the one who acts.

Fanon's notion of man re-creating himself through violence has raised a controversy among commentators. Some, like Aimé Césaire, conceive of the notion of humanistic violence as "non-violent violence." In a passage, quoted earlier, Césaire writes:

> But his violence, and this is not paradoxical, was that of the non-violent. By this I mean the violence of justice, of purity and of intransigence. This must be understood about him.[27]

But the fact that it is the violence of justice, violence committed in the name, or in the pursuit, of justice does not make it nonviolent. Violence advocated to achieve the aims of nonviolence is still violence, and no amount of poetic juggling of words can escape this fact. Another possible suggestion is that Fanon's notion of purificatory violence is in fact metaphysical violence and that he is thinking along the lines of Camus when he (Camus) talks of metaphysical rebellion.[28] A close reading of Fanon, however, does not bear this out. David Caute also calls Fanon's violence "non-violent violence,"[29] but he restricts this to Fanon's early views on violence, which he calls an "existential view of violence." Gendzier, however, denies the notion of humanistic violence:

> The statement that Fanon was a humanist of violence and an optimist has often appeared to be excessive, illusory, or simply

> dishonest. After all it was attributed to a man who made violence a critical feature of his world policy.[30]

Later she writes: "It is this aspect of his concept of violence which, so graphically expressive in words, is considerably less convincing as a policy."[31]

It is possible for the initial spontaneous violence of the colonized against the colonizer to have this purificatory effect. The colonized has for a long time been fed on the myth of the superiority of the colonizer. In the first act of spontaneous violence against the colonizer, the colonized for the first time sees the colonizer running away in fear and fright, or begging for his life, or undergoing indignities at the hands of the colonized to save his life. The colonized then comes to a sudden realization that the colonizer is after all human like himself, and that he has the same weaknesses, fear, and anxieties as anyone else. The myths begin to fall, and it is at this point that the colonized is said to "vomit" back all the values of the colonizer. At this point he loses all his inferiority and regains his self-confidence and manhood. It is in this sense that one should seek to understand Fanon's concept of the purificatory role of violence. This is the violence that changes consciousness and personality. Yoweri T. Museveni, who did fieldwork among the armed guerillas in Mozambique, has unearthed evidence that supports Fanon's thesis and throws much light on the whole notion of the emancipatory role of violence. He writes:

> Another aspect of the revolution, which I do not think could have come about except as a result of the revolutionary armed struggle, is the liberation of the peasant from not only his previous inferiority complexes but also from his parochialism. . . . The peasant in Cabo Delgado has participated in killing the white man—the former "demi-god." He has inflicted defeat on this "god." The white "god," the colonialist, has been seen and known to wriggle in an agony of death from bullets fired by guns operated by peasants. The peasants have set mines which have

> blown to pieces white soldiers. The erstwhile "gods" have been seen to fly like startled warthogs before the automatic fire by peasant guerrillas. They have been captured by peasants; they have put up their arms in supplication for mercy from their former slaves—the natives. . . . The white man—the invulnerable god—will be seen vomiting, shivering and expressing anxiety about what he considers imminent death.[32]

In this light, to talk of the emancipatory role of violence is not to engage in metaphysics or illusion, or dishonesty, as Gendzier suggests. But it is possible to argue that this emancipatory role of violence is true only in the short run, and that to have a lasting effect this initial violence has to be accompanied by political education.

Fanon's discourse on the emancipatory role of violence poses a number of problems. First, he is not as unequivocal about violence for the liberation of consciousness as he appears. Even in the *The Wretched of the Earth*, where the insistence on violence takes a lyrical form, Fanon writes:

> If we have taken the example of Algeria to illustrate our subject, it is not at all with the intention of glorifying our own people, but simply to show the important part played by the war in leading them towards consciousness of themselves. *It is clear that other peoples have come to the same conclusion in different ways. We know for sure today that in Algeria the test of force was inevitable; but other countries through political action and through the work of clarification undertaken by a party have led their people to the same results.*[33] (Emphasis added.)

From the above it seems that it is possible to achieve liberation of consciousness through political education or by mental contemplation. That violence is not the only way to achieve liberation of consciousness is evidenced from the experiences of Marx, Lenin, and a host of other revolutionaries. We know that Fanon himself did not play any combat role in the Algerian revolution. How did he acquire his revolutionary consciousness? Or is one to argue that it is not so much the use of violence that is critical in the emancipation of consciousness as the readiness to use violence?

Another problem with the emancipatory role of violence is that violence does not always lead to the freeing of the individual from his fears and inferiority complexes. On the contrary, it sometimes leads to neurosis and distortion of personality, as Fanon himself recognizes.[34]

It is significant to note that Fanon produces examples from both the oppressed and the oppressor group to indicate the effect of violence on the personality. Let us take one example: the case of the man with vertigo. As a member of the movement for armed struggle against the colonialists, this man had planted a bomb in a café frequented by arch racists. There was no feeling of revenge about the act. It was ordered by his superiors to counteract the terror and violence of the colonialists. It is an act that would be regarded as perfectly justifiable within the framework or the norms of revolutionary violence. He himself had no qualms about the act at the time of commission, nor did he repudiate it afterward. The bomb had killed ten people. Afterward, the man began to suffer from vertigo. At a certain date each year (the date he had planted the bomb) he suffered from "prolonged insomnia, accompanied by anxiety and suicidal obsessions."[35] Fanon's own comments on the case are instructive:

> The circumstances surrounding the appearances of these disorders are interesting for several reasons. Some months after his country's independence was declared, he had made the acquaintance of certain nationals of the former colonial power, and he had found them very likeable. These men and women greeted the new independent state warmly and paid tribute to the courage of the patriots who had fought in the struggle for national freedom. The former militant therefore had what might be called an attack of vertigo. He wondered with a feeling of anguish whether among the victims of the bomb there had been people like his new acquaintances. It was true that the café that it was aimed at was

a meeting-place for notorious racists; but there was nothing to prevent a quite ordinary passer-by going in and having a drink.[36]

How do we explain this? If we accept that this maladjustment was the direct result of participation in violence, then we cannot avoid the conclusion that violence, even revolutionary violence, both emancipates and alienates. If that is the case, the critical question then becomes, On what conditions does revolutionary violence emancipate and on what conditions does it alienate? Are there any personalities whom it alienates? If so, on what personalities does violence act as a liberating force and on what does it act as an alienating force? The answers to these questions would provide the key to the understanding of the complex issues connected with Fanon's discussion on the emancipatory role of violence. It could be argued, of course, that the whole notion of emancipatory violence in Fanon is a myth.[37] Although no serious critic would deny the presence of certain mythmaking in Fanon, it would be wrong to dismiss the entire argument as a myth. Besides, if the main purpose of this is to create a myth, it is difficult to understand the inclusion of material that casts so much doubt on his own myth. Is Fanon trying to warn us that however justified revolutionary violence might be, one cannot avoid the consequences of certain actions?

violence as a dialectical necessity

Another reason that Fanon advances to justify his argument for the emancipatory role of violence is that it is the colonizer who initially introduces violence into the relationship between the settler and the native. We are not told the origin of the settler's violence. Presumably, it is part and parcel of the capitalist society, where alienation is the feature of each person's life and where each person treats the other as an object. The violence of the colonizer is used not only to exploit the material wealth of the colonies but to dehumanize the native. The initial violence of the settler is the thesis, and here one has to remember that, according to Fanon, the initial contact between the settler and the native is always marked by violence. This violence of the settler creates an antithesis, the violence of the native, but against himself. For some time the native turns the violence on himself, but then a point is reached "when daily life becomes impossible."[38] The native then responds to the settler's violence with violence. Fanon writes:

> The violence of the colonial regime and the counter-violence of the native balance each other and respond to each other in an extra-ordinary reciprocal homogeneity. This reign of violence will be the more terrible in proportion to the size of the implantation from the mother country.[39]

The bigger the settler community is, the more pervasive and intense the violence is. Hence, the response of the native is also more intense. The native's response to the colonizer's violence with violence against the colonizer constitutes the synthesis and a resolution of the dialectic. The native regains his humanity through the use of violence and frees himself from the domination of the settler. Fanon's use of the dialectic differs from Marxist usage. Here the dialectic that progresses by conflict is not set into motion as a result of the disharmonious relations between the forces of production and the relations of production. It is the will and the consciousness of the individual that set the dialectic in motion. Sometimes Fanon gives the impression that this will be an instinctive reaction to an intolerable situation:

> For the Negro who works on a sugar plantation . . . there is only one solution: to fight. He will embark on this struggle . . . not as a result of a Marxist or idealist analysis but quite simply because he cannot conceive of life otherwise than in the form of a battle against exploitation, misery, and hunger.[40]

violence as an instrument for creating solidarity

According to Fanon, it is not enough for the colonized to gain liberation of consciousness. The social and political institutions of the colonial regime ought to be completely destroyed, and new ones created. In order to destroy these structures effectively, it is necessary to build solidarity among the colonized, and he sees violence as playing an important role in the building of this solidarity. Violence, he says, represents absolute praxis. It is an act of commitment. It is an irrevocable act. It binds the people together to form a collective individual. Fanon writes:

> In Algeria, for example, where almost all the men who called on the people to join in the national struggle were condemned to death or searched for by the French police, confidence was proportional to the hopelessness of each case. You could be sure of a new recruit when he could no longer go back into the colonial system. This mechanism, it seems, had existed in Kenya among the Mau-Mau, who required that each member of the group should strike a blow at the victim. Each one was thus personally responsible for the death of that victim. . . . This assumed responsibility for violence allows both strayed and outlawed members of the group to come back again and to find their place once more, to become integrated.[41]

Fanon continues:

> The practice of violence binds them together as a whole, since each individual forms a violent link in the great chain, a part of the great organism of violence which has surged upwards in reaction to the settler's violence in the beginning. The groups recognize each other and the future nation is already indivisible. The armed struggle mobilizes the people: that is to say, it throws them in one way and in one direction.[42]

The armed conflict creates a feeling of solidarity and introduces into the consciousness of the people the idea of a "common cause, of a national destiny and of a collective history."[43] Colonial rule is separatist rule. It stresses ethnic differentiation and sets one ethnic group against the other. The townspeople are also set against the rural people. In such a situation each individual is pitched against the other. We have already discussed how the violence, oppression, and cultural dehumanization of the colonial regime create a feeling of self-hatred in the native. This affects his relations with other natives. These relations are marked by violence, since, being unable to turn the violence on the colonizer, he turns it upon himself. Writing about Algeria, Fanon says: "The Algerians rob each other, cut each other up and kill each other."[44] During the armed struggle for liberation this violence is channeled into the fight, and a marked departure from interpersonal violence among the natives is noticed. Here again Fanon relates the experience of Algeria:

> It has been established that since 1954 crimes in common law have almost disappeared. There are no more disputes and no longer any insignificant details which entail the death of a man. There are no longer explosive outbursts of rage because my wife's forehead or her left shoulder were seen by my neighbour. The national conflict seems to have canalized all anger, and nationalized all affective or emotional movements.[45]

Museveni relates the same phenomenon among the Mozambican fighters:

> In the case of Cabo Delgado, not only have there been no murders since the beginning of the revolution but even petty fights have perceptibly disappeared. For instance, I carried out investigations in two military bases, but I did not come across any case of fighting among either the fighters or civilians within a year.[46]

It is common knowledge that in times of crisis people sink their differences and come together to face the common danger. This, however, depends on whether or not the individuals have fundamentally different perceptions of what constitutes a common danger. Sometimes the armed struggle, far from creating solidarity, creates conflicts among the combatants. Armed guerrillas in Angola sometimes expend more energy fighting other rival guerrilla groups than fighting the oppressor.

violence as an instrument for effective decolonization

As we have seen from the above, violence is not only necessary for creating new men but also for breaking the political and social institutions of the colonial society and building new ones. Although Fanon generally tends to see the independence struggle and the decolonization process going hand in hand as a single struggle, in some cases he sees a separation of the two into a first phase of political independence and a second phase of decolonization. In this case the first phase could be achieved without a violent struggle.

> All the colonial countries that are waging the struggle today must know that the political independence that they will wring from the enemy in exchange for the maintenance of an economic dependency is only a snare and a delusion, that the second phase of total liberation is necessary because required by the popular masses, that this second phase, because it is a capital one, is bound to be hard and waged with iron determination. . . .[47]

If this interpretation of the two-stage revolution (which Fanon's own model rejects) is accepted, then it means that for certain countries it is possible to work for a negotiated nonviolent political independence, and then launch the drive for "total liberation" later. This later "total liberation" is the liberation of both the country and the individual. In this case political independence will be pursued as a necessary precondition for the second stage of total decolonization. And it is in this context that Fanon writes: "If need be the native can accept a compromise with colonialism, but never a surrender of principle."[48]

This strategy would be possible if the country in question had "progressive and enlightened" (not Fanon's words) leadership that would propel the nation to the second stage, which would involve a complete dismantling of the colonial structures. Is it possible to achieve this without any violence? Fanon argues that a colonial power never withdraws unless completely defeated or when there is a chance of continuing to wield influence. We shall therefore assume that in the case of negotiated independence the colonial powers agree to this only with the full knowledge that they can keep their interests well protected. If this is the case, one would expect the ex-colonial power to resist, and to respond with violence if necessary, when the local elites attempt to change the political and social structures in such a way as to achieve decolonization. And in fact Fanon insists that the social revolution that is the decolonization process will always be a violent confrontation. He argues in the manner of Régis Debray on the necessity of armed combat to raise consciousness.[49] But he also admits that it is not in all cases that violence is necessary to raise consciousness. He admits that in some cases the initial task of raising consciousness could be undertaken by the party.[50] This, however, is not the actual decolonization process, which is still a violent confrontation. However, the success that Tanzania seems to be having in its attempts to achieve decolonization and build a socialist society would seem to indicate that perhaps the two-stage decolonization process could work under "enlightened" leadership, and the second stage could come about without any violence. It is nevertheless too early to make any decisive judgment on the Tanzanian experiment.[51]

agencies of revolutionary violence

We have seen Fanon's justification for the use of revolutionary violence for decolonization.[52] But revolutionary violence has to be employed by individuals or groups, and Fanon turns next to a discussion of the roles of the various social groups in a revolution.

Looking at the situation in the Third World, Fanon identifies four main social classes and discusses the potential of each class for revolutionary decolonization. Although he does not define his social classes[53] in any precise terms, he characterizes them in such a way as to make them easily identifiable.

The four main groups he identifies are the national bourgeoisie, the urban proletariat, the peasants, and the lumpen-proletariat. He does not define any of these groups; he only characterizes them.

The national bourgeoisie refers to the group usually called the middle class.[54] It occupies the top layer of the social structure in African societies, and consists of men of the liberal professions, the administrative bourgeoisie, landowners, and a few men of commerce. The proletariat constitutes the urban working class, and in their ranks are to be found tram conductors, taxi-drivers, miners, dockers, interpreters, nurses, and so on.[55] The peasants are the small cultivators whose surplus value is exploited by the big farmers, the urban population, and the state generally. Contrary to the argument of some who accuse Fanon of treating the rural population as an undifferentiated mass, Fanon does in fact make distinctions between the peasantry as such and the rich farmers.[56] Admittedly, he does not stratify the rural population in any detailed way as Mao does in his study of the Hunan province;[57] but a clear distinction is made, however, between peasants and rich farmers who occupy the same class position as the national bourgeoisie.

By the lumpen-proletariat Fanon means the urban unemployed or unemployables. These are "the pimps, the hooligans, the unemployed and the petty criminals."[58] Among them are also the prostitutes and "all the hopeless dregs of humanity."[59]

the role of the national bourgeoisie

Marx pays generous tribute to the bourgeoisie of Europe for breaking the back of the feudal society and taking a leading role in the movement that built industrial capitalism in the nineteenth century, though he castigates them for their regressive role in the capitalist society. In the *Manifesto of the Communist Party* he writes:

> The bourgeoisie, historically, has played a most revolutionary part. . . .
>
> The bourgeoisie, during its rule of scarce one hundred years, has created more massive and more colossal productive forces than have all preceding generations together. Subjection of nature's forces to man, machinery, application of chemistry to industry and agriculture, steam navigation, railways, electric telegraphs, clearing of whole continents for cultivation, canalization of rivers, whole populations conjured out of the ground—what earlier century had even a presentiment that such productive forces slumbered in the lap of social labor?[60]

Fanon argues that in the underdeveloped countries the bourgeoisie has not even played this initial role.

> The national middle class which takes over power at the end of the colonial regime is an under-developed middle class. It has practically no economic power, and in any case it is in no way commensurate with the bourgeoisie of the mother country which it hopes to replace. . . . The university and merchant classes which make up the most enlightened section of the new state are in fact characterized by the smallness of their number and their being concentrated in the capital, and the type of activities in which they are engaged: business, agriculture and the liberal professions. Neither financiers nor industrial magnates are to be found within this national middle class. The national bourgeoisie of under-developed countries is not engaged in production, nor in invention, nor building, nor labour; it is completely canalized into activities of the intermediary type. Its innermost vocation seems to be to keep in the running and to be part of the racket. The psychology of the national bourgeoisie is that of the businessman, not that of a captain of industry.[61]

The immediate reason for such a sad state of affairs is that the bourgeoisie not only lacks a developmental ethic but is also steeped in indulgence and conspicuous consumption.

> In the colonial countries, the spirit of indulgence is dominant at the core of the bourgeoisie; and this is because the national bourgeoisie identifies itself with the Western bourgeoisie, from whom it has learnt its lessons. It follows the Western bourgeoisie along its path of negation and decadence without ever having emulated it in its first stages of exploration and invention.[62]

Fanon argues that this sort of behavior is symptomatic not only of the bourgeoisie of the urban areas. It is also a feature of its class allies, the big farmers.[63] The national bourgeoisie also lacks initiative, imagination, and entrepreneurial skills, qualities indispensable for achieving decolonization. It is conspicuous in its inability to make use of the techniques learned in European universities to solve local problems. Moreover, it has failed to provide effective leadership in the important function of achieving national unity and nation-building.

Another reason why the national bourgeoisie of the underdeveloped countries fails to play a progressive role in the decolonization process is its slavish imitation of European patterns of thought and its unquestioning assimilation of ideas to which it was exposed during its training in European universities. For example, it imports the notion of the political party from abroad and tries to apply it mechanically in Africa:

> The notion of the party is a notion imported from the mother country. This instrument of modern political warfare is thrown down just as it is, without the slightest modification, upon real life with all its infinite variations and lack of balance, where slavery, serfdom, barter, a skilled working class and high finance exist side by side.[64]

Another example of its lack of imagination and creative intellect is the undue attention paid to the urban working class in slavish imitation of the European mass parties.

Furthermore, the national bourgeoisie develops an ideology of nonviolence. It is not clear whether this springs from its own feeling of inferiority vis-à-vis the white rulers, and here the story of Bigger Thomas in Richard Wright's *Native Son* is instructive, or from a conviction that in such a context violence is suicidal, or both. Whatever the case, it disassociates itself from spontaneous violent movements that, if it had the imagination and the correct analysis of the African situation, it would support and thus channel its enthusiasm and energy into more profitable ends. Given the Fanonist argument that revolutionary violence is the only way to freedom, the fact that the national bourgeoisie shuns anti-colonial violence rules it out as an effective leadership group for decolonization. Commenting on this attitude of the bourgeoisie, Fanon states:

> He loudly proclaims that he has nothing to do with these Mau-Mau, these terrorists, these throat-slitters. At best, he shuts himself off in a no-man's-land between the terrorists and the settlers and willingly offers his services as go-between; that is to say, that as the settlers cannot discuss terms with these Mau-Mau, he himself will be quite willing to begin negotiations.[65]

Another reason that the national bourgeoisie of the underdeveloped countries does not take a positive role in the decolonization process is its intellectual laziness.

> This traditional weakness, which is almost congenital to the national consciousness of under-developed countries, is not solely the result of the mutilation of the colonized people by the colonial regime. It is also the result of the intellectual laziness of the national middle class, of its spiritual penury, and of the profoundly cosmopolitan mould that its mind is set in.[66]

Among progressive intellectuals, Fanon is unique in his negative characterization of the developmental roles of the bourgeoisie of the underdeveloped countries. Considering the evidence adduced by Fanon, it is amazing that other writers have perceived the situation differently. How do we account for this difference?

In 1960 Edward Shils published an article on the role of the intellectuals in the developing countries, in which he attributed a positive role to them. Transferring the European framework to the developing nations, he wrote:

> Modern revolutionary politics have been a domain very much reserved for intellectuals. . . .
>
> The prominence of intellectuals in the politics of the new states of Asia and Africa arises in part from the special affinity which exists between the modern intellectual orientation and the practice of revolutionary or unconstitutional politics. . . .[67]

Looking at the situation in Africa, it is difficult to agree with Edward Shils's contention unless the word *revolutionary* is equated with unconstitutional politics. Even so, the period of unconstitutional politics was extremely short. Other writers have followed the same trend, attributing positive roles to the national bourgeoisie.[68] This is because the national bourgeoisie was in the forefront of the independence race, and its progressive role was taken for granted. Besides, in the perspective of some of these writers, the capture of the national state or the Africanization of the colonial authority is equated with decolonization. For Fanon decolonization involves not merely taking over the colonial state apparatus, or Africanization of the local bureaucracy and its authority structure, but structural and institutional changes in the society that lead to the creation of "new men" and new relationships. So far, this revolutionary transformation has not occurred, nor does the current role of the national bourgeoisie lead one to expect this kind of change. Hence Fanon's indictment.

For the reasons mentioned above, Fanon concludes that the national bourgeoisie is incapable of playing a "progressive" role in decolonization, and urges its abolition.

In spite of the powerful indictment, Fanon's argument about the role of the national bourgeoisie in revolutionary decolonization raises a number of questions, not because his diagnosis is wrong, but because some of his assumptions are questionable. Although only the most recalcitrant will now deny class formation in Africa, it is doubtful whether in reality class formation has reached the point of such sharp distinctions as Fanon's analysis seems to assume. In Africa, because of the nature of kinship relations and ethnicity compounded by patron-client relations, the bourgeoisie is not always perceived to stand in such sharp contrast with the rest of society as Fanon's analysis suggests.[69] Of course, it can be argued that the lower classes have "false consciousness," but the crucial question is the perceptual images that they hold of the bourgeoisie. And here the evidence does not suggest that they always view them as class enemies, nor do they see their interests as always antagonistic to those of the bourgeoisie.[70]

Fanon's analysis also assumes that the national bourgeoisie has a common interest, and he does not envisage the possibility of conflict among this group.[71] Is it not possible for the revolutionary intellectuals to form an alliance with a section of the national bourgeoisie to provide effective leadership for decolonization?[72] Fanon argues that due to the nature of the socialization process of the bourgeoisie, it will not be able to take a progressive role in decolonization. If this were so, we would not expect people like Marx, Lenin, and Fanon himself to overcome their socialization and assume revolutionary roles. It has to be conceded, however, that though it is possible for certain individual members of the bourgeoisie to overcome their class origins and socialization process and assume revolutionary roles, for the bourgeoisie as a class such a radical transformation cannot be envisaged.

Fanon's attitude toward the national bourgeoisie is also ambivalent. On the one hand, he urges its abolition because of its weaknesses; but on the other hand, he exhorts it to play a progressive role in the decolonization process, which indicates that he admits that it is possible for the national bourgeoisie to overcome its "false consciousness." The basis of this thinking is to be found in his idea of man in relation to his environment. He argues that the individual is determined, but not completely, by the environment. With will, courage, and determination he can transcend his existential condition, and it is on account of this that he castigates the national bourgeoisie of the underdeveloped countries.

the role of the urban working class

> Of all the classes that stand face to face with the bourgeoisie today, the proletariat alone is a really revolutionary class.[73]

Marx regarded the proletariat, the urban working class, as the most revolutionary class, because it is the most organized, the most alienated, and the most class-conscious. Socialist revolutions have on this account always concentrated on the urban working class as the backbone of the revolution. So much has this become part of Marxist ideology that even when departures are made, the rhetoric of the workers' revolution is still maintained.

The leaders of the underdeveloped areas, especially in Africa, try to replicate the European notion of the workers' party in their own countries. In many African countries much of the political action against the colonial powers took place in the main cities, with the urban working or non-working class forming the backbone of the mass parties and the national movements that rose to challenge the colonial presence. On account of this the working class has been wrongly equated with its European counterpart as a revolutionary class.[74]

Fanon, however, argues that the revolutionary nature of the proletariat is related to the specific historical conditions of Europe and cannot be translated wholesale into the African situation. The African proletariat does not resemble the proletariat of Europe. It is in fact a *petite bourgeoisie* with a stake in the colonial system; it occupies a privileged position; and it is too small. Fanon also argues that the working class of the underdeveloped countries performs the same tasks as the European proletariat, but has been subject to *embourgeoisement*:

> . . . tram conductors, taxi-drivers, miners, dockers, interpreters, nurses and so on. It is these elements which constitute the most faithful followers of the nationalist parties, and who because of the privileged place which they hold in the colonial system constitute also the "bourgeois" fraction of the colonized people.[75]

So strongly does Fanon feel about this that he stresses it again and again.

> It cannot be too strongly stressed that in the colonial territories the proletariat is the nucleus of the colonized population which has been most pampered by the colonial regime. The embryonic proletariat of the towns is in a comparatively privileged position. In capitalist countries, the working class has nothing to lose; it is they who in the long run have everything to gain. In the colonial countries the working class has everything to lose; in reality it represents that fraction of the colonized nation which is necessary and irreplaceable if the colonial machine is to run smoothly.[76]

> . . . The working class in the colonies is in an embryonic state and represents that fraction of the people which is the most favoured.[77]
>
> . . . For the workers are in fact the most favoured section of the population, and represent the most comfortably off fraction of the people.[78]

The proletariat also has the same class interests as the national bourgeoisie. It is only interested in taking and maintaining the privileges left by the whites and not in radical changes in the society.

> Their way of thinking is already marked in many points by the comparatively well-to-do class, distinguished by technical advances, that they spring from. Here "modern ideas" reign.[79]

On account of the above weakness, he concludes that the African proletariat is incapable of taking an effective role in the revolutionary violence necessary for decolonization. He argues that the mistake of African political leaders in the area of political organization was to have approached this "wrong" class:

> The great mistake, the inherent defect in the majority of political parties in under-developed regions has been, following traditional lines, to approach in the first place those elements which are the most politically conscious: the working classes in the towns, the skilled workers and the civil servants—that is to say, a tiny portion of the population, which hardly represents more than one per cent.[80]

One of the immediate questions that strikes one on reading Fanon's discourse on the urban working class is the absence of a precise delineation of the group. Without clearly defining it, he tells us that it includes tram conductors, taxi-drivers, miners, dockers, interpreters, nurses, and so on. If we take the social class as a group of people marked off by their socioeconomic status and the place they occupy in the mode of production and certain modes of behavior, we cannot lump interpreters, nurses, dockers, or miners together as forming a single working class. On this point Fanon has drawn a sharpe rebuke from Nguyen Nghe:

> Il y a d'abord erreur à ranger dans la même classe sociale les dockers et mineurs avec les interprètes et les infirmiers. Les premiers constituent le prolétariat vrai, la classe ouvrière industrielle (dans les colonies, il faut aussi ranger dans cette classe les ouvriers des grandes plantations); les seconds font partie de la petite-bourgeoisie, elle aussi révolutionnaire, mais avec moins de résolution et d'esprit de suite.[81]

This inability or unwillingness to define the social classes clearly mars Fanon's analysis somewhat and makes interpretation rather difficult.[82] G. Arrighi and J. Saul have also characterized the African working class as polarized into two strata. The lower stratum is only partly proletarianized and is close to the peasantry, whereas the upper stratum, the "labor aristocracy,"[83] forms part of the elite or the sub-elite. Viewed in this way, Fanon's argument has validity.

Another point that Fanon raises is that in the underdeveloped countries the proletariat is rather small due to the underdeveloped nature of the capitalist economy. On account of this it does not make good sense to use as a backbone of the revolution a group that represents only a tiny fraction of the population. Numbers, however, should not be of prime importance. Instead one should place a premium on "correct ideological perspective," the strategic position in the production process, political consciousness, and the will to fight. Besides, Fanon has stated also that the working class is the most "politically conscious." One would think that effective strategy would demand the use of those who are the most politically conscious, since all one would do would be to direct them to the "correct" ideological position. It should be remembered that one of the main reasons that Marx rejects the peasantry in favor of the proletariat is the former's lack of political consciousness.

Fanon is not alone, though he was probably the first to claim that the urban working class in Africa is pampered and enjoys a privileged position.[84] Modibo Keita of Mali says of the African working class and its living standards: "We know that they [i.e., the working class] were not the most exploited when they had work."[85] Senghor also thinks that the living wages of the urban working class put them far above the peasants. Evidence from the reports of various commissions set up in both the colonial and post-colonial era on the wage scales of urban workers indicates, however, that the living standards of urban workers are far from desirable.[86] A report submitted to the Minimum Wages Board from Kivukoni College, Tanzania, for instance says:

> In the cases explained none of the workers were receiving a sufficient income to support themselves with absolute necessities and a healthy diet, let alone support a family, and in practically every case investigated workers were supporting fully or partly other people in addition to their own wives and children. Their debts were incurred overwhelmingly to pay for necessities.[87]

If we are to maintain the differentiation suggested by Saul and Arrighi, this would express the position of most of the lower-stratum workers.

The experience of the Tanzanian workers can be repeated in many areas of Africa. Quite apart from earning low wages, workers are often only in seasonal employment. Besides, they also have to support hangers-on, job-seekers, and others claiming kinship ties.[88] In view of this, there are others who are prepared to argue that the African urban worker is not in a privileged position. Urban workers even in the upper stratum may not be as pampered as Fanon claims; but compared with the rural peasantry, they are still better off. Much has been made of the fact that they do share their wages with their rural kin, but one has to remember that this flow of money and material benefits is not in one direction only, i.e., from the urban workers to the rural kinfolk. The rural kin also send gifts in the form of farm products to their relatives in the urban areas. It is true that sometimes the urban workers have to support dependents, but here also these dependents sometimes perform domestic work far above the cost of their keep.[89] Furthermore, the urban workers depend on their kinsmen in the rural areas in times of sickness or other mishaps. Ousmane Sembene, in his novel *God's Bits of Wood*, discusses the dependence of the railway workers on their kinfolk in the rural areas during a prolonged strike.[90]

So the dependence is mutual. The African worker does not have the anxiety of the American worker about sickness. He knows that when he is sick his kinsmen will take care of him and pay whatever medical expenses are necessary until he gets well. The question, however, is not whether the urban worker is pampered but whether he is better off as compared with the peasant. The evidence points to the fact that he is better off than his rural counterpart; moreover, he sees himself as better off.

The more crucial question, however, is whether the fact that the working class is better off prevents it from developing a revolutionary consciousness. Most revolutions are led by middle-class intellectuals, counter-elites whose standard of living is comparatively higher than the majority of the population. And usually those who are most anxious to join revolutionary movements are not economically the most depressed part of the population. People who join revolutionary movements more often than not do so out of their perceived chances of improving their conditions. For those who are so depressed that they cannot even conceive of a better life, the chances of participating in revolutionary movements do not recommend themselves to them. When they do engage in violence or acts of rebellion against authority, it is more to maintain a certain pattern or mode of existence than to achieve a revolutionary transformation of society, unless their predisposition to violence is given a revolutionary direction by their being subjected to some form of political education or consciousness-raising. Besides, another potent force that impels men to take a revolutionary position is a deep sense of moral commitment.

Finally, Fanon says that the workers have "political consciousness." He even concedes that the urban working class played an important role during the fight for independence.

> During the colonial phase, the nationalist trade-union organizations constitute an impressive striking power. In the towns, the trade unionist can bring to a standstill, or at any rate slow down at any given moment, the colonialist economy. Since the European settlement is often confined to the towns, the psychological effects of demonstrations on that settlement are considerable: there is no electricity, no gas, the dustbins are left unemptied, and goods rot on the quays.[91]

Is it not possible that through political education organized by the revolutionary intellectuals the working class could be made to develop revolutionary consciousness, and thus become an effective force in decolonization? It is surprising that Fanon does not consider this possibility.

the role of the peasantry

After discounting the national bourgeoisie and the urban working class, Fanon settles on the peasantry as the most revolutionary class. Why does he regard the peasantry of the underdeveloped countries as the most revolutionary? He thinks it has certain particular attributes that predispose it to revolutionary action. The peasantry, in its stern determination to maintain the social structure of the precolonial society, remains the most "disciplined element" of the population. Fanon concedes that the stubborn determination of the peasantry to maintain the social structure may sometimes give rise "to movements which are based on religious fanaticism or tribal wars."[92] However, it is in this determination and spontaneity that its strength lies.

> But in their spontaneous movements the country people as a whole remain disciplined and altruistic. The individual stands aside in favour of the community.[93]

It is much easier to arouse the peasants to political consciousness, since they have not suffered alienation as have the urban working class and the national bourgeoisie. They have not been made to feel inferior, and they have not sunk to that psychological state of a feeling of impotence or of nonbeing. In addition, in their folklore the anti-colonial struggle still looms large in a form that is not distorted by the colonizer.

The peasants are also supposed to be "pure." They live in close contact with their traditional societies and are not corrupted by Westernization. "[They] keep their moral values and their devotion to the nation intact."[94] They are also generous and ready to sacrifice themselves completely.[95] They have pride and confidence in themselves, and are "rebels by instinct."[96] They are the only people who have managed to maintain their individuality in the face of the colonialist onslaught.

> From all eternity, by means of manifold tricks and through a system of checks and balances reminiscent of a conjurer's most successful sleight-of-hand, *the country people had more or less kept their individuality free from colonial imposition.*[97] (Emphasis added.)

Fanon also argues (though Sartre makes the point more forcefully) that what contributes to the revolutionary potential of the peasant is his economic deprivation and suffering:

> For it [the peasantry] knows naked oppression, and suffers far more from it than the workers in the towns, and in order not to die of hunger, it demands no less than a complete demolishing of all existing structures.[98]

For all these reasons Fanon considers the peasants as the "only spontaneously revolutionary force."[99] In fact, inverting Marx's dictum, he says the peasants alone are revolutionary.[100]

Of the revolutionaries who regard the peasantry as revolutionary, the one whose ideas are closest to Fanon's is Michael Bakunin. Like Fanon, he also argues that in Eastern Europe, where the proletarian stratum was lacking, the peasantry constituted the chief revolutionary force. Like Fanon also, he characterizes the peasantry as pure, integrated, and oppressed, factors that in his view predispose to revolutionary action. He writes:

> [The peasants] can be stirred into action, and sooner or later they will be stirred by the social revolution. This is true for three reasons: a) Owing to their backward or relatively *barbarous* civilization, they have retained in all integrity the simple robust temperament and the energy germane to the folk nature. b) They live from the labor of their hands, and are morally conditioned by this labor, which fosters an instinctive hatred for all the privileged parasites of the state, and for all the exploiters of labor. c) Finally, being toilers themselves, they share common interests with the city workers, from whom they are separated by their prejudices.[101]

Mao also regards the peasants as the most revolutionary group:

> . . . *It was they* [the peasants] *who fought, who organized, and who did the revolutionary work. They alone* are the deadliest enemies of the local bullies and evil gentry . . . *they alone are able to carry out the work of destruction. . . .*[102]

Unlike Fanon, however, Mao's main reason for regarding the peasants as the most revolutionary is economic. They are the most exploited class.

Lin Piao, Mao's former chief disciple has gone further than any other in glorifying the peasantry. He extends his idealization of the peasantry to the village, which he regards in opposition to the city as the only base for revolutionary action.

> The village, and the village alone, is the boundless, vast field of action for revolutionaries. The village, and the village alone, is the revolutionary base from which revolutionaries set out on a march to win final victory.[103]

Lin Piao also goes on to characterize the industrialized nations as the "city" and the Third World nations as the "village," thereby imputing that it is only from the Third World that revolutionary action can come. Régis Debray's thinking also comes close to that of Lin Piao. He regards the city as the center of *embourgeoisement*, which has to be avoided:

> . . . Any man, even a comrade, who spends life in a city is unwittingly bourgeois in comparison with a *guerrilero*. . . .[104]

He continues:

> As we know, the mountain proletarianizes the bourgeois and peasant elements, and the city can bourgeoisify the proletarians.[105]

René Dumont, the French agronomist, also shares the view of the revolutionary potential of the peasantry, whom he calls "proletarians of modern times."[106] Even Marx recognizes that in certain situations the peasants could be the majority of the toiling people and not the proletarians.[107] In such a case it is natural for them to be the revolutionary vanguard. It is argued by Fanon that such a situation obtains in the Third World.

It must be remembered that the above qualities with which Fanon endows the peasantry apply only to this group in the underdeveloped countries. Drawing a distinction between the European peasantry and the peasantry in the underdeveloped countries, Fanon agrees with Marx about the European peasantry being "the least aware," "the worst organized," and "the most anarchic."

> They show a whole range of characteristics—individualism, lack of discipline, liking for money and propensities towards waves of uncontrollable rage and deep discouragement which define a line of behavior that is objectively reactionary.[108]

In addition, the peasantry also "constitutes a brake on the revolution."[109]

The question to consider now is whether the peasant has the attributes that Fanon assigns to him and, if so, whether such attributes necessarily predispose to revolutionary action. When Fanon attributes discipline to the peasant, what does he mean? By discipline, is he referring to the propensity of the peasant to follow his leaders and chiefs; and if so, how does this constitute a revolutionary potentiality? The chiefs and leaders of the peasants are perhaps some of the most conservative elements in African society, and we would not think that a propensity to follow them necessarily implies revolutionary action. If, on the other hand, by the most disciplined element Fanon means the most strong-willed or the most fanatical, then this is a source of strength. To be a successful revolutionary, it is necessary to be fanatical as far as goals are concerned, and flexible as far as tactics are concerned. He also claims that the peasants of the underdeveloped countries, unlike the urban working class, are not individualistic and have great social solidarity. Agrarian people usually have a greater sense of communality than urban people, but we also know that in certain parts of Africa the peasants are scattered and live in isolated homesteads. Mahjemout Diop, writing about Senegal, says:

> The peasants are mostly illiterate, unorganized and dispersed among 12,000 villages and rural townships. Primitive forms of production and organization and the superstructure corresponding to these forms lag far behind the requirements of the modern world, owing to which *the winning of the peasantry in* active struggle as the natural ally of the working class will obviously be a difficult task for some time to come.[110]

Tanzania's problems in organizing peasants living in isolated homesteads into villages is an illustration of the extreme difficulties involved in organizing the peasantry. Besides, the case is not as clear as Fanon would have us believe. Within each kin group or in each small community there is an intense human relationship and a feeling of belonging to the group, but this does not extend to other groups.[111] The problem would be how to transfer this intense feeling that each peasant has for his immediate group to other groups or to the nation-state. This intense feeling for one's fellow man is not an intrinsic quality of the peasant, but is characteristic of all social groups in small communities who live in intimate face-to-face relations with each other. Factory workers living in intimate relations with each other also develop such ties of solidarity. Besides, the intensity of human relationships is a function of the limited scale of interaction that characterizes peasant existence. Once the scale of interaction is expanded, it will not be possible to maintain the same intensity of human relationships. The intensity of human relationships therefore is not an intrinsic quality of the peasantry.

Fanon also claims that the peasantry lives in close contact with his society and keeps his moral values intact. He is not alienated from his culture. He is, in a word, integrated. All the evidence we have from the sociological literature indicates that the one who is integrated is less likely to revolt or indulge in revolutionary activity than the one who is alienated and who lives on the fringes of the culture. Innovations are nearly always caused by marginal men. The integrated always have reasons to explain their adverse conditions: it is the will of the gods, or some other fatalistic reason; but the alienated is more likely to blame either himself or the one he thinks responsible for his condition, and to do something about it.[112]

Fanon also credits the peasants with kindness, generosity, and devotion to the nation. It would be difficult to persuade anyone that kindness and generosity are either one revolutionary qualities or that such qualities predispose to revolutionary activities. It is possible that people who have shared dangers together will develop strong comradeship for each other, but this is the result of their intense involvement with each other. It is the result, not the cause, of revolutionary activity. Would the peasant extend the same kindness that he shows toward members of his ethnic and kin groups to other groups with which he would have to be in contact? The same question can be asked about the peasant's devotion to the nation. The peasant is devoted, but not to the nation. His mental horizon does not go beyond the limits of his immediate social group. The peasant is also thought to be endowed with feelings of self-confidence and moral superiority vis-à-vis the colonizer. Whereas a sense of self-confidence could be an asset for revolutionary action, it is conceivable that a feeling of moral superiority on the part of the peasant would be more likely to generate a feeling of contemptuous disregard of the colonizer than a determination to fight him.

The peasant is supposed to have a propensity for violence, and Fanon thinks this is an asset for revolutionary activity. He describes the peasants as "rebels by instinct," and those "who never cease to think of the problem of their liberation except in terms of violence." It is difficult to conceive of "rebels by instinct" as being at the same time the "most disciplined." One may concede that the peasant has a propensity to respond with violence when his interests are threatened. The peasant base of the Mau Mau, and the recourse to arms by the cocoa farmers of Ghana to protect their cocoa trees from being cut down are cases in point. However, to show a propensity for violence to protect one's own interests is one thing, and to engage in revolutionary violence is another.[113] Nguyen Nghe argues that even when the peasant engages in armed struggle, he does not follow it through to seek the structural changes in the society that revolution entails. After the struggle is over, he returns to his old habits.

> Nous avons vu au Vietnam d'anciens combattants de la Résistance, revenir aprés neuf années de maquis, à leur fumerie d'opium; nous avons vu des paysans qui avaient fait la guerilla pendant des années, avoir peur à nouveau des fantômes, parce que s'était ébranlée la confiance politique dans le parti qui les dirigeait, à la suite des erreurs commises au cours de la réforme agraire.[114]

To be a revolutionary, the peasant has to cultivate revolutionary consciousness; and for this, political education is necessary. Nghe writes:

> Le paysan, de lui-même, ne peut jamais avoir une conscience révolutionnaire; c'est le militant venu des villes qui devra détecter patiemment les éléments les plus doués dans la paysannerie pauvre, faire leur éducation, les organiser, et c'est seulement après une longue période de travail politique qu'on peut mobiliser la paysannerie.[115]

We may argue that Nghe has misunderstood Fanon, and that, although Fanon seems to be saying so, he does not really imply that the peasant develops a revolutionary consciousness by himself. This is supposed to be the work of the urban militants and the revolutionary intellectuals. On this both Fanon and Nghe are in agreement. The confusion arises as a result of carelessness in Fanon's own writing. At one point he describes the peasants as "spontaneously revolutionary" and the "only revolutionary class," but his own model of revolutionary warfare shows clearly that it is the revolutionary intellectuals from the urban centers who desert the city and take off to the rural areas and the mountains who do the initial work of raising the revolutionary consciousness of the peasantry. All that Fanon is entitled to claim by the logic of his own argument is that the peasants constitute a potentially revolutionary class.

The second part of Nghe's argument about Vietnamese peasants who return to their old habits of smoking opium after nine years in the *maquis* underlies this. Peasants do not automatically become revolutionary. This argument is also buttressed by the observations of David and Marina Ottaway of the Algerian peasantry:

> The peasants, for their part, have not proven to be as revolutionary as they were during the war of independence. They have not agitated to obtain an agrarian reform or to force the government to give more attention to their problems.[116]

They also add that the peasants have returned to their old ways. A more recent work by Marie Perinbam also concludes:

> With few notable exceptions—most of which come from the *autogestion* sector—the post-independence reactions of the peasants have been less than revolutionary.[117]

The empirical evidence, then, does not seem to support Fanon when he writes, as he sometimes does, that mere participation in armed struggle is enough to revolutionize the peasant. A careful reading of the text, however, reveals that Fanon is much more careful than he is sometimes given credit for being. Participation in armed struggle has the immediate effect of releasing the peasant from his feeling of inferiority with respect to his oppressor. But for such a process of regeneration and revolutionizing to take place on a permanent basis, it must be accompanied at all times by political education.

> It is not only necessary to fight for the liberty of your people. You must also teach that people once again, and first learn once again yourself, what is the full stature of a man; *and this you must do for as long as the fight lasts.*[118] (Emphasis added.)

We may add that this must be continued even after the fight. For it is only in this way that the colonized can be brought to the realization of his full stature and measure as a man.

Amilcar Cabral, whose credentials as a revolutionary were unquestionable, did not share Fanon's view of the peasantry as the main revolutionary force.

> Here I should like to broach one key problem, which is of enormous importance for us, as we are a country of peasants, and that is the problem of whether or not the peasantry represents the main revolutionary force. I shall confine myself to my own country, Guinea, where it must be said at once that the peasantry is not a revolutionary force—which may seem strange, particularly as we have based the whole of our armed liberation struggle on the peasantry. A distinction must be drawn between a physical force and a revolutionary force; physically, the peasantry is a great force in Guinea: it is almost the whole of the population, it controls the nation's wealth, it is the peasantry which produces; but we know from experience what trouble we had convincing the peasantry to fight.[119]

This is a far cry from Fanon's "the peasant masses will always answer the call to rebellion."[120] Here we agree with Amilcar Cabral. The peasant may have a propensity for violence, and may have great physical force, but these qualities in themselves do not make him revolutionary. This point is also recognized by Robert Buijtenhuijs in his study of the Mau Mau in Kenya. He writes:

> Third-World peasant masses are perhaps the first to think that only violence pays—the Mau Mau combattants demonstrated this.

However, to be ready to use violence does not mean that one has a consciousness of revolution. . . .[121]

Besides, as Cabral has pointed out, the fact that the peasantry does not constitute the main revolutionary force does not mean the revolutionary movement cannot be based on the peasantry. It still represents a great physical force.

As we have already remarked, Fanon gives the impression that it is the revolutionary intellectuals from the urban areas who lead the revolutionary fight. It is a union between the revolutionary intellectuals from the city and the peasants that results in the embryonic political organization.[122] In spite of this initial impression he creates, Fanon adds that the peasants will come to show that they are capable of directing the people's struggle.[123] This idea of the peasant's directing the struggle has provoked unfavorable attention from certain critics, who insist that it is the urban militants or the urban working class who direct the people's struggle. Nguyen Nghe quotes approvingly from Troung Chinh, a theoretician of the Vietnamese revolution, to substantiate his criticism of Fanon.

> Quant à la force motrice de la révolution, elle est constituée par la classe ouvrière, la classe paysanne, la petite bourgeoisie. Le rôle dirigeant revient à la classe ouvrière. La classe des paysans travailleurs forme la principale armée de la révolution. La petite-bourgeoisie et la bourgeoisie nationale sont les alliés de la classe ouvrière, avec cette différence toutefois que la bourgeoisie nationale est un allié conditionnel.[124]

Nghe himself, arguing powerfully against Fanon, writes:

> Le paysan pauvre peut être un patriote et mourir héroïquement fusil en main, mais s'il reste un paysan, il ne saurait diriger le mouvement révolutionnaire. Il faut soigneusement distinguer entre les forces motrices de la révolution et celles qui la dirigent. Il y avait tout au long de l'histoire des révoltes paysannes, des

> jacqueries qui finissaient toujours dans l'anarchie ou au profit d'éléments féodaux. Jamais encore, des paysans pauvres n'avaient pu mener à bien une révolution pour leur propre compte.[125]

He continues:

> Car la révolution qui doit s'opérer dans les pays coloniaux à l'heure actuelle n'est pas seulement nationale; elle doit être moderne. Cette dimension moderne ne peut être conçue par la paysannerie; elle ne peut être apportée au pays que par la bourgeoisie ou la classe ouvrière.[126]

Jack Woddis, also arguing strongly against Fanon's position, follows Engels's argument that the peasant alone cannot succeed in a revolutionary war and that he needs a class ally.[127] The peasant, Woddis argues, has been a powerful force against feudalism and imperialism, but has never been able to achieve a major victory on his own. It is only when the peasant is in alliance with, and under the leadership of, the bourgeoisie, as was the case in the French Revolution of 1789, or in alliance with, or led by, the working class, as was the case with the Russian Revolution of 1917, that success can come.

This criticism, however, is based on a misinterpretation of Fanon. It is true that Fanon says that the peasants alone are revolutionary, but he does not argue that the revolution must be made by the peasants and the peasants alone. It is logical that if the peasants alone are revolutionary, then they should prosecute the revolutionary war alone. But Fanon does not argue along such lines. He sees the revolutionary war as an alliance of the revolutionary intellectuals, the peasants, and, as we shall see below, the lumpen-proletariat. Thus, far from rejecting alliances, he accepts them, but not from the urban working class or the national bourgeoisie. Nghe's strictures against Fanon, powerful though they are, are in some cases also based on a misinterpretation of Fanon. We agree with Nghe when he argues that the peasant by himself cannot develop revolutionary consciousness; but when he begins to argue that it is the urban militant who leads the fight, and who ought to lead, we do not see much difference between his position and Fanon's. Fanon does not say that it is the peasant who leads, or ought to lead, the fight. He says it will be found that the peasant is capable of directing the people's fight.[128] Fanon's statement should be understood as arguing that peasants have capabilities for leadership and a plea that they should not be dismissed on *a priori* grounds from leadership positions.

In sum, we can say that the attributes that Fanon gives to the peasant do not necessarily predispose him to revolutionary action. This is not to deny that the peasant could play an important role in a revolutionary movement. We know, for instance, what critical roles the peasants have played and are still playing in the revolutionary movements in China, Vietnam, Cuba, and Mozambique. The crucial question then becomes, Under what conditions do the peasants participate in revolutionary action? Also, what strata of the peasant population are most prone to revolutionary action? Fanon's inability to stratify the peasantry beyond the broad distinctions of rich and poor peasant, to assess the revolutionary potential of each stratum, and to delineate clearly the conditions under which each stratum could become predisposed to revolutionary warfare are major weaknesses in his argument. In this connection the writings of Eric Wolf and Hamza Alavi have contributed immensely to our understanding of this phenomenon.[129]

the role of the lumpen-proletariat

Another group of people that Fanon regards as revolutionary and that should be allied to the peasantry in the revolution is the lumpen-proletariat. These are the urban unemployed or unemployables whom we have mentioned above. These consist of peasants who have left the rural life for the city, but who have not become part of the social system of the city. They form a "horde of starving men, uprooted from their tribe and from their clan."[130] They live on the fringes of the city in the "shanty towns."[131] Fanon regards them as

> the men whom the growing population of the country districts and colonial expropriation have brought to desert their family holdings circle tirelessly around the different towns, hoping that one day or another they will be allowed inside.[132]

They are located in almost every major city in Africa—Dakar, Abidjan, Accra, Lagos, Nairobi, Kinshasha, and Johannesburg. Among this group can also be found those born and raised in the city who have only tenuous or no rural roots.

Marx and his disciples treat the lumpen-proletariat with suspicion and sometimes with contempt. In the *Manifesto of the Communist Party*, Marx and Engels refer to it as that " 'dangerous class', the social scum, that passively rotting mass thrown off by the lowest layers of old society."[133]

In *The Class Struggles in France* Marx argues that the lumpen-proletariat in all big towns "forms a mass sharply differentiated from the industrial proletariat." He goes on to characterize it as a

> recruiting ground for thieves and criminals of all kinds, living on the crumbs of society, people without a definite trade, vagabonds, *gens sans feu et sans aveu*, varying according to the degree of civilization of the nation to which they belong, but never renouncing their *lazzaroni* character.[134]

Engels, in a preface to *The Peasant War in Germany* writes:

> The lumpen-proletariat, this scum of the depraved elements from all classes, with headquarters in the big cities, is the worst of all

> possible allies. This rabble is absolutely venal and absolutely brazen. . . . Every leader of the workers who uses these scoundrels as guards or relies on them for support proves himself by this action alone a traitor to the movement.[135]

It would thus seem that for Marx and Engels, the lumpen-proletariat is thoroughly unreliable and worthless. However, in spite of this negative characterization, Marx claims in *The Class Struggles in France* that the lumpen-proletariat is "thoroughly malleable, as capable of the most heroic deeds and the most exalted sacrifices as of the basest banditry and the foulest corruption."[136] This is supposed to be its character in its "youthful stage."[137] This means that it could play a positive role in the revolution, if advantage is taken of its malleability.

In his analysis of the role of the lumpen-proletariat, Lenin dwells on its tendency to engage in spontaneous and disorganized action, armed struggle against the state, and in the taking over of state property. Lenin, however, also recognizes what Marx earlier noted about the lumpen-proletariat: if they could be controlled, they would serve a positive purpose for the revolution. Hence he castigates those who write them off summarily, and contends that it is not actions of such nature that disorganize the struggle, but the inability of a party to take advantage of such actions and bring them under its control. He goes on to say that the Bolsheviks must organize these spontaneous acts and train and prepare their organizations to be able to act as a belligerent side that does not miss a single opportunity for inflicting damage to the enemy's forces.[138]

Mao's views on the lumpen-proletariat are also very similar:

> . . . There is a fairly large number of lumpen-proletarians, that is, peasants who have lost their lands and handicraftsmen who have lost all opportunity of employment. They lead the most precarious kind of life. . . . To assign these people to their proper

> role is one of China's difficult problems. *Able to fight very bravely but apt to be destructive, they can become a revolutionary force when properly guided.*[139] (Emphasis added.)

Unlike Engels, he does not dismiss them completely.

Fanon, following Marx, Lenin, and Mao, also recognizes the revolutionary potential of the lumpen-proletariat. His enthusiasm for them as a revolutionary force is almost as great as that for the peasantry. He writes:

> It is within this mass of humanity, this people of the shanty towns, at the core of the lumpen-proletariat that the rebellion will find its urban spearhead. For the lumpen-proletariat . . . *constitutes one of the most spontaneous and the most radically revolutionary forces of a colonized people.*[140] (Emphasis added.)

Why does Fanon regard the lumpen-proletariat as a revolutionary force? As in the case of the peasantry, he endows them with "revolutionary" qualities. Like the peasantry they have a propensity for violence, and for Fanon violence is indispensable for revolution. They also have tenacity, will, and courage: "This lumpen-proletariat is like a horde of rats; you may kick them and throw stones at them, but despite your efforts they'll go on gnawing at the roots of the tree."[141] In addition to their propensity for violence, they live in social conditions that predispose them to react violently against the system, i.e., the colonial system. It is "that fraction which has not yet succeeded in finding a bone to gnaw in the colonial system."[142] Here we have the prostitutes and the maids who are paid 2,000 francs (about six dollars) a month, but the majority are usually unemployed people who live on the fringes of the city. Not being a part of the countryside, where they have been "uprooted from their tribe and from their clan,"[143] they do not form part of the urban culture, and they show hostility to established social norms. They live in what Fred Riggs describes as a state of "normlessness,"[144] or better still, by their own norms. In such a situation they live by their wits and are entirely opportunistic, seeking their ends by any and every means. And in this state, violence comes most readily. But this predisposition to violence is useful only if it can be controlled and channeled into revolutionary activity. Fanon is quite aware that the lumpen-proletariat could be a destructive force used against the revolution. In fact, this is one of the reasons why he urges the revolutionary movement to gain control of it before its enemies do. He writes:

> Colonialism will also find in the *lumpen-proletariat* a considerable space for manoeuvring. For this reason any movement for freedom ought to give its fullest attention to this *lumpen-proletariat*. The peasant masses will always answer the call to rebellion, but if the rebellion's leaders think it will be able to develop without taking the masses into consideration, the *lumpen-proletariat* will throw itself into the battle and will take part in the conflict—but this time on the side of the oppressor. And the oppressor, who never loses a chance of setting the niggers against each other, will be extremely skilful in using that ignorance and incomprehension which are the weaknesses of the *lumpen-proletariat*. If this available reserve of human effort is not immediately organized by the forces of rebellion, it will find itself fighting as hired soldiers side by side with the colonial troops.[145]

One may ask how the destructive potential of the lumpen-proletariat is overcome after the revolution. Would it not constitute a problem for the new regime? Fanon's answer is that the lumpen-proletariat is reformed through the process of revolution, and discovers its "true" humanity.

> So the pimps, the hooligans, the unemployed and the petty criminals, urged on from behind, throw themselves into the struggle for liberation like stout workingmen. These classless idlers will by militant and decisive action discover the path that leads to nationhood. They won't become reformed characters to please colonial society, fitting in with the morality of its rulers; quite on the contrary, they take for granted the impossibility of their enter-

> ing the city save by hand-grenades and revolvers. These workless less-than-men are rehabilitated in their own eyes and in the eyes of history. The prostitutes too, and the maids who are paid two pounds a month, all the hopeless dregs of humanity, all who turn in circles between suicide and madness will recover their balance, once more go forward, and march proudly in the great procession of the awakened nation.[146]

Fanon's discourse on the lumpen-proletariat has raised considerable controversy, and a number of objections have been made against his argument. Robin Cohen and David Michael cast doubts on the notion of a revolutionary lumpen-proletariat.

> That the lumpen-proletariat has participated in collective expressions of dissent is not in question. One may cite popular demonstrations in support of strikers, tax riots in Western Nigeria, or celebrations after the downfall of an unpopular government. In no case that we know of, however, have the lumpen-proletariat played a major, let alone, initiatory role.[147]

African politicians have made use of the urban unemployed in their struggle against the colonial regime and also against their local rivals. Nkrumah's "verandah boys," the "Action Troopers" of Kumasi,[148] and Azikiwe's "Zikist Movement"[149] are only a few examples. Since most of the African mass parties are urban-based, the support of this urban non-working class is considerable. The role of these people in precipitating the 1965 Western Nigeria crisis that foreshadowed the military coup is far from insignificant. That they have not played any role in revolutionary violence is due to the fact that the African political leadership has not channeled their energies into such pursuits. Furthermore, Fanon's argument is not that the lumpen-proletariat should play the initiatory role, as Robin Cohen and David Michael suggest, but that it constitutes a reservoir of energy that, if tapped, would provide the urban spearhead of the revolution. The initiatory role is for the revolutionary intellectuals. It is important to remember that Fanon describes the lumpen-proletariat as "urged on from behind."

Another question is the marginality of the urban lumpen-proletariat. Fanon argues that the lumpen-proletariate lives on the fringes of the urban social system. It is not really part of the urban culture, and at the same time it is not as integrated into the rural culture as the peasants who continue to live on the land. Robin Cohen and David Michael challenge the concept of the alienated lumpen-proletariat.

> The lumpen proletariat are much less alienated from the neo-colonial economy than the Fanonists imply. Many of them, indeed, have an important stake in the system and live, like parasites, off the productive labor of others—whether it be through dependence on the income of employed kin, through theft or through the provision of services like prostitution.[150]

For Fanon, the lumpen-proletariat is "that fraction which has not yet succeeded in finding a bone to gnaw in the colonial system." Presumably, once they find a bone, they cease to be lumpen-proletarians; they become proletarians proper. How can people who do not have a bone to gnaw in the system have a stake in the system, as Robin Cohen and David Michael claim? All the evidence we have indicates that the lumpen-proletariat has alternated between support for the reactionaries and support for the revolutionaries. If any proof is needed to support the view that they have no stake in the system, it is this.

The debate on the lumpen-proletariat is further clouded by the fact that, just as in the case of the peasantry, neither Fanon nor his critics make any distinctions in the structure of the urban unemployed.[151] Peter Gutkind differentiates two main elements, the "unemployed" and the "unemployables." The unemployed are those semiskilled men who have been in employment and lost their jobs for a variety of reasons; they occupy one end of the spectrum. At the other extreme are the "unemployables," the infirm and those unwilling or unable to hold any job. Within these extremes there may be other categories of unemployed, such as juveniles, those without any schooling or with only primary education, the seasonally unemployed, and those who seek better jobs than the ones they had before. In addition to these are the "raw" migrants who have difficulty finding jobs, being recent arrivals and not experienced in the ways of the urban setting. In spite of this differentiation, Gutkind argues, the unemployed as a collective category exist on the margins of African urban society.[152] From this it is clear that sometimes when a writer designates attributes to the urban unemployed, the attributes may apply only to one category of the unemployed. It is this failure to differentiate clearly the structure of this group that has created the confusion. Fanon himself lumps together the recent arrivals and the hard-core lumpen-proletariat. However, the recent arrivals are qualitatively different from the hard-core lumpen-proletariat: the latter are the pimps, the hooligans, and the criminals. They have hardly any contact with the rural world, nor are they all from the rural areas. Normally, one would expect this group to show a greater propensity for violence, and therefore to be useful raw materials for revolution. The recent arrivals, on the other hand, often live with their kin, and are to some extent anchored within the social system of the immediate kinship structure. There is one thing that both groups have in common: they both live on the fringes of the urban social system.

Amilcar Cabral, a more careful writer, has delineated such groups and has assessed the revolutionary potential of each:

> Then in the towns there are rootless people who may also be divided, and into two groups. One of these two groups does not

> really deserve the name of "rootless", but we have yet to find a better term for them. The other group is easily identified, and might be called our lumpen-proletariat, if we had anything in Guiné which we could properly call a proletariat: they consist of beggars, lay-abouts, prostitutes etc.
>
> Now it is on the first of these two "rootless" groups that we have concentrated particular attention, and it is a fact that they have played a very important part in our liberation struggle. They consist of a large number of young folk lately come from the countryside, and retaining links with it, who are at the same time beginning to live a European sort of life. They are usually without any training and live at the expense of their petty-bourgeois or labouring families.[153]

It is worth noting that for Cabral it is the new arrivals who have been most useful. For the hard-core lumpen-proletariat, Cabral had no use. This is perhaps less because they could not be used for revolutionary activity than because of the seriousness of the risks involved.

Robin Cohen and David Michael also argue that the lumpen-proletariat has no consciousness of itself as a class, is unable to identify its enemies in class terms; and furthermore, there is not as big a gap between them and the proletarians proper as Fanon's argument implies. This criticism is also based on a view of the lumpen-proletariat as a monolithic group. We have already indicated the different social categories that make up the urban lumpen-proletariat. According to Gutkind, when the recent arrivals have difficulty getting jobs, tension arises between them and their relatives or kin group with whom they live. They then move on to other relatives till they have in this way exhausted all their kin group, and then they move to stay with their friends. Gutkind writes:

> When a job seeker has thus reached the stage when employers treat him as unemployable, and his relatives and friends no longer offer him dependable aid, he is relegated to a new social milieu. The network of his contacts and associations, his friends and the social groups he selects, now comprise predominantly other unem-

ployed men. While he will continue to visit his working friends and relatives, the greater part of his time is spent on activities no longer designed to help him find employment.[154]

The unemployables begin to manifest signs of class consciousness as they begin to interpret their predicament in class terms.[155] These are the ones who become the pimps, the criminals, and the hooligans. These are the people who "endanger the 'security' of the town."[156] The fact that they support either the conservatives or the revolutionaries is more an indication of their cynicism than their lack of class consciousness or inability to define their class enemies.

Fanon's notion of the lumpen-proletariat being reformed through revolutionary violence raises a number of problems. The lumpen-proletariat, as we know already, has a strong predisposition to violence, and it does indulge in acts of violence. If it is the act of violence that purifies it, why is it not purified by the daily acts of violence that it commits? Fanon could argue that there is a difference between its daily acts of violence and revolutionary violence, which is directed against a system that oppresses it. But as we have already seen, it is possible for even revolutionary violence to produce alienation. Furthermore, Fanon states that the lumpen-proletariat could fight on either side. If that is the case, why should it fight on the side of the revolutionaries? Is it because fighting affords it the chance to express its violence, or because it becomes committed to the cause of the revolutionaries? If it fights on account of the former reason, then it is difficult to see how such participation in violence could liberate its consciousness. If, on the other hand, it fights on account of the latter reason, then it means its conversion precedes its participation in revolutionary violence. We do not deny that the lumpen-proletariat could participate in revolutionary violence, but that such participation would revolutionize it is rather difficult to conceive.

It is possible for certain members of the lumpen-proletariat to be converted to revolutionary consciousness. We have the experiences of Malcolm X, Eldridge Cleaver, George Jackson, and a number of Black Panther members to support this. Malcolm X, Eldridge Cleaver, and George Jackson, however, did not acquire their revolutionary consciousness through armed conflict. They changed through intense mental contemplation made possible by long periods of confinement in prison. Interestingly enough, after their conversion they all claimed the necessity for violence to achieve liberation.

Fanon's argument about the lumpen-proletariat is that it has certain qualities and lives in a certain social condition that predisposes it to the use of violence. This violence could be controlled and channeled to revolutionary activities. And to the extent that Fanon considers violence a necessary part of revolution, he sees the lumpen-proletariat as potential revolutionaries. He therefore urges an alliance between it and the peasantry. The claims of critics that the lumpen-proletariat has not played any initiating or major role, or that it has often supported conservative politicians, do not invalidate Fanon's argument. A much more serious criticism that can be made of Fanon, especially in his role as a revolutionary intellectual, is his failure to stratify the urban unemployed and to assess the revolutionary potential of each stratum, indicating the conditions in which each could be drawn into the revolutionary process. And it is this sensitivity to the subtlety and complexity of the urban unemployed that gives added significance to the writings of Amilcar Cabral. One can say that Cabral carried Fanon's analysis one step further.

The above discusses and analyzes the roles of various classes in revolutionary violence. As we have seen, Fanon does not define his social classes, and his characterization of them is far from satisfactory. His analysis assumes a sharp class division of African society. It is not that class analysis is wrong, but it has to be refined to provide explanatory insight into the nature of African politics. In Africa, ethnicity, kinship, and patron-client relations mediate, but do not necessarily vitiate, class conflict; and any inquiry into the structure of African politics using class as an analytical category should take this into consideration. Fanon is ambivalent in his treatment of the national bourgeoisie, and his characterization of the peasantry is wanting in certain respects. His arguments for the rejection of the proletariat as a revolutionary force are based on a simplistic view of the proletariat as an undifferentiated mass; and it is the same simplistic view that leads him to characterize the entire lumpen-proletariat as revolutionary.

As much as we may find particular aspects of his thinking faulty, his argument taken in its totality has a great deal of force; and when the necessary qualifications are made to some of his statements, the core of his argument will not be found to be lacking in profundity or originality. His genius lies in his ability to discern the revolutionary potential of certain social classes previously neglected and to make a passionate argument for a complete rethinking of the strategy for revolutionary decolonization.

Fanon's interest is not only in the liberation of man but also in prescribing political and social arrangements that will enable man to maintain and to express his freedom won through the revolutionary struggle.

1. Some of the important works are: Jerome A. Shaffer, ed., *Violence* (New York: David McKay, 1971); Hannah Arendt, *On Violence* (New York: Harcourt, Brace & World, 1969); Hannah Arendt, "Reflections on Violence," *New York Review of Books* 12 (February 1969), pp. 19-31; Robert Paul Wolff, "On Violence," *Journal of Philosophy* 66 (October 1969), pp. 601-16; J. Glen Gray, *On Understanding Violence Philosophically and Other Essays* (New York: Harper & Row, 1970); Hannah Arendt, *On Revolution* (New York: Viking Press, 1965); Krishnan Kumar, *Revolution* (London: Weidenfeld & Nicolson, 1971); Peter Calvert, *Revolution* (London: Pall Mall, 1970); Chalmers Johnson, *Revolutionary Change* (Boston: Little, Brown & Co., 1966); Samuel Huntington, *Political Order in Changing Societies* (New

Haven, Conn.: Yale University Press, 1968); *Comparative Politics*: Special Issue on Revolution, vol. 5, no. 3 (April 1973); Isaac Kramnic, "Reflections on Revolution: Definition and Explanation in Recent Scholarship," *History and Theory: Studies in Philosophy of History* 2 (1972): 26–63; Michael Freeman, "Review Article: Theories of Revolution," *British Journal of Political Science* 2 (1972): 339-59; Perez Zagorin, "Theories of Revolution in Contemporary Historiography," *Political Science Quarterly* 88 (March 1973): 23-52; W. F. Wertheim, *Evolution and Revolution* (Harmondsworth, Middlesex: Penguin Books, 1974).

2. Fanon, *The Wretched of the Earth*, p. 28.

3. Ibid., p. 29.

4. Ibid., p. 56.

5. Ibid., p. 57.

6. Ibid., p. 61.

7. Ibid., p. 64.

8. Barbara Deming, "On Revolution and Equilibrium," *Liberation* 12 (February 1968): 11.

9. Martin Staniland, "Fanon and the African Political Class," *African Affairs*, January 1966, p. 12.

10. Aristide R. Zolberg, "Frantz Fanon: Gospel for the Damned," *Encounter* 27 (November 1966): 62.

11. Karl Kautsky, *The Social Revolution*, quoted in Kramnic, "Reflections on Revolution," p. 26.

12. Even in this, Fanon is not very consistent. In the first chapter of *The Wretched of the Earth*, he uses the term *decolonization* to indicate revolutionary transformation of a colonial society, without which there can be no authentic liberation. In contrast to independence, which in essence does not bring any benefits to the people but merely a change in the racial composition of the government, he writes: "But it is a commonplace to observe and to say that in the majority of cases, for ninety-five percent of the population of under-developed countries, independence brings no immediate change" (*The Wretched of the Earth*, p. 59).

On the other hand, he sometimes uses the term *decolonization* to indicate a condition of mere independence, and uses the term *independence* to indicate total disengagement from colonialism. It is in this sense that he says the FLN does not aim at achieving decolonization but independence: "The FLN does not aim at achieving a decolonization of Algeria or a relaxation of the oppressive structure. What the FLN demands is the independence of Algeria. An independence which will allow the Algerian people to take its destiny wholly in hand" (*Toward the African Revolution*, p. 101).

For the purposes of uniformity we shall keep *decolonization* for revolutionary transformation of the colonial society and *independence* for the replacing of colonial elites with native elites.

13. For a discussion of the concept of a political revolution, see Eugene Kamenka, "The Concept of a Political Revolution," in Carl Friederich, ed., *Revolution* (New York: Atherton, 1964).

14. Herbert Marcuse, "Ethics and Revolution," in Richard T. De George, ed., *Ethics and Society* (Garden City, N.Y.: Doubleday, 1966), p. 134.

15. Certain writers talk of nonviolent revolution; see Susan Hacker, "Violent and Non-Violent Approaches to Revolution," *Mawazo* 3 (June 1972): 1-11.

16. Fanon, *The Wretched of the Earth*, p. 27.

17. Ibid.

18. Ibid., p. 28. Here we come across one of the problems involved in the interpretation of Fanon, i.e., lack of clarity. The French "la chose colonisée," translated as "the thing colonized" or "the colonized thing" or "the thing which has been colonized," seems to give the impression that the "thing" exists prior to colonization; but it is colonization that produces the "thing."

19. Ibid.

20. Ibid.

21. Ibid., p. 237.

22. *Black Skin, White Masks*, p. 198; in *The Wretched of the Earth* the quotation appears on page 69.

23. The emancipatory violence can be either of a purely individual nature or of a collective nature.

24. Fanon, *The Wretched of the Earth*, p. 74.

25. Jean-Paul Sartre, *Iron in the Soul* (London: Hamish Hamilton, 1950), p. 245; originally published in French as *La Mort dans l'âme*.

26. Richard Wright, *Native Son* (1940; rpt. New York: New American Library, 1964), pp. 224-25.

27. "Homage to Frantz Fanon," *Présence Africaine*, vol. 12, no. 40 (1962), pp. 131-32.

28. Albert Camus, *The Rebel* (New York: Vintage Books, 1956).

29. Caute, *Fanon*, p. 81.

30. *Frantz Fanon*, p. 3.

31. Ibid., p. 198.

32. Yoweri T. Museveni, "Fanon's Theory on Violence: Its Verification in Liberated Mozambique," in Nathan Shamuyarira, ed., *Essays on the Liberation of Southern Africa* (Dar-es-Salaam: Tanzania Publishing House, 1971), p. 14.

33. P. 155.

34. Ibid., pp. 200-236.

35. Ibid., p. 203.

36. Ibid., footnote.

37. Two scholars have tried to interpret Fanon in this way, though not necessarily in connection with his writing on violence: Marie Perinbam, "Fanon and the Revolutionary Peasantry: The Algerian Case," *Journal of Modern African Studies* 2 (1973): 427-45; Barbara Abrash, "Frantz Fanon: The Political Philosopher as a Mythmaker," in Emmanuel Hansen and Adele Jinadu, eds., *Frantz Fanon: The Man, His Work, and His Thought* (forthcoming).

38. Fanon, *The Wretched of the Earth*, p. 69.

39. Ibid.

40. *Black Skin, White Masks*, p. 224.

41. *The Wretched of the Earth*, p. 67.

42. Ibid., p. 73.

43. Ibid.

44. Ibid., p. 247. Alvin Poussaint has also noticed this phemenon among blacks in the United States; see *Why Blacks Kill Blacks*.

45. *The Wretched of the Earth*, p. 247.

46. "Fanon's Theory on Violence," p. 13.

47. Fanon, *Toward the African Revolution*, p. 125-26.

48. *The Wretched of the Earth*, p. 114.

49. Régis Debray, *Revolution in the Revolution?* (New York: Grove Press, 1967).

50. Fanon, *The Wretched of the Earth*, p. 155.

51. As some of the observers of the Tanzanian scene have pointed out, there are serious contradictions in the Tanzanian political system the resolution of which might entail violence. See Issa G. Shivji, *The Silent Class Struggle* (Dar-es-Salaam: Tanzania Publishing House, 1973), pp. 1-60; Issa G. Shivji, "The Silent Class Struggle Continues," mimeographed (Dar-es-Salaam, 1972); John Saul, "African Peasants and Revolution," *Review of African Political Economy*, No. 1 (1974), pp. 41-68.

52. One writer has found in Fanon an ethical justification of revolutionary violence; see Jesse Nathaniel McDade, "Frantz Fanon: The Ethical Justification of Revolution" (Ph. D. diss., Boston University, 1970).

53. For the literature on social classes in Africa, see Immanuel Wallerstein, "Class and Class Conflict in Contemporary Africa," *Canadian Journal of African Studies* 7 (1973): 375-80; R. H. Jackson, "Political Stratification in Tropical Africa," *Canadian Journal of African Studies* 7 (1973): 381-400; Szymon Chodak, "Social Stratification in Sub-saharan Africa," *Canadian Journal of African Studies* 7 (1973): 401-17; Robin Cohen, "Class in Africa: Analytical Problems and Perspectives," *Socialist Register*, 1972, pp. 231-55; Samir Amin, *The Class Struggle in Africa* (Cambridge, Mass.: Africa Research Group, n.d.); Kwame Nkrumah, *Class Struggle in Africa* (New York: International Publishers, 1970); Szymon Chodak, "Social Classes in Sub saharan Africa," *Africana Bulletin*, No. 4 (1966), pp. 7-46; Kenneth Grundy, "The 'Class Struggle' in Africa: An Examination of Conflicting Theories," *Journal of Modern African Studies* 2 (November 1964): 379-93.

54. This term is not particularly appropriate in the African situation because there is no upper class. We may ask: middle between what and what? Ledda also objects to the term *national bourgeoisie*; see his "Social Classes and Political Struggle," *International Socialist Journal*, No. 22 (August 1967), p. 566.

55. Fanon, *The Wretched of the Earth*, p. 86.

56. Ibid., p. 124.

57. Mao Tse-Tung, *Analysis of the Classes in Chinese Society* (Peking: Foreign Languages Press, 1956). See also "An Analysis of the Various Classes of the Chinese Peasantry and Their Attitudes toward Revolution," in S. Schram, *The Political Thought of Mao Tse-Tung* (New York: Praeger, 1969), pp. 241-46.

58. Fanon, *The Wretched of the Earth*, p. 103.

59. Ibid., p. 104.

60. *Manifesto of the Communist Party*, in Feuer, *Marx and Engels*, pp. 9, 12.

61. *The Wretched of the Earth*, pp. 119-20.

62. Ibid., p. 123.

63. Ibid., p. 124.

64. Ibid., p. 85.

65. Ibid., p. 49. Anyone who has carefully observed the activities of the so-called African middle-class leaders during the fight for independence will appreciate the poignancy of Fanon's statement.

66. Ibid., p. 119.

67. Edward Shils, "The Intellectuals in the Political Development of the New States," *World Politics* 12 (1960): 300.

68. James Coleman, *Nigeria: Background to Nationalism*; Ruth S. Morgenthau, *Political Parties in French-Speaking West Africa*.

69. See Martin Kilson, "African Political Change and the Modernization Process," *Journal of Modern African Studies* 1 (1963): 425-40.

70. This point is well illustrated in Chinua Achebe's novel *Man of the People* (London: Heinemann, 1966).

71. Conflicts of interest between the political leadership and the intellectuals were quite frequent in Ghana during the Nkrumah regime.

72. W. F. Wertheim sees in this strategy a real possibility for revolutionary transformation of society; see *Evolution and Revolution*, pp. 262-63.

73. *Manifesto of the Communist Party*, in Feuer, *Marx and Engels*, p. 17.

74. There are writers who even question whether the American and West European working class as presently constituted is in fact revolutionary; see Herbert Marcuse, *One Dimensional Man* (Boston: Beacon Press, 1966).

75. *The Wretched of the Earth*, p. 86.

76. Ibid.

77. Ibid., p. 96.

78. Ibid., p. 97.

79. Ibid., p. 86.

80. Ibid.

81. Nguyen Nghe, "Frantz Fanon et les problèmes de l'indépendance," *La Pensée*, February 1963, p. 30. "First of all there is a mistake in putting in the same social class dockers and miners together with interpreters and nurses. The first make up the proletariat proper, the industrial working class (in the colonies it is also necessary to include in this class the plantation workers); the second make up part of the *petite bourgeoisie*. It is also revolutionary, but it has less determination and enduring spirit."

82. For an attempt to define the working class in Africa, see V. L. Allen, "The Meaning of the Working Class in Africa," *Journal of Modern African Studies* 10 (1972): 169-89.

83. G. Arrighi and J. Saul, "Nationalism and Revolution in Sub-Saharan Africa," *Socialist Register*, 1966, p. 158.

84. There is very little empirical evidence to fall back upon, but others who have argued in similar terms are: Julius Nyerere, *Ujamaa: Essays on Socialism* (Dar-es-Salaam: Oxford University Press, 1968), pp. 27-28; W. Arthur Lewis, *Reflections on Nigeria's Economic Growth* (Paris: Development Centre of the OECD, 1967), p. 42; Peter Kilby, *Industrialization in an Open Economy: Nigeria, 1945-66* (Cambridge: At the University Press, 1969), p. 301; Elliot Berg, "Major Issues of Wage Policy in Africa," in A. M. Ross, ed., *Industrial Relations and Economic Development* (London: Macmillan, 1966), p. 189. Others who have also recently added their voices to the debate on labor aristocracy and the revolutionary or nonrevolutionary nature of the working class are: Jack Woddis, *New Theories of Revolution* (New

York: International Publishers, 1972); Raphael Kaplinsky, "Myths about the 'Revolutionary Proletariat' in Developing Countries," *Institute of Development Studies* (Sussex University), vol. 3 (August 1971), pp. 15-21; Keith Hinchliffe, "Labour Aristocracy: A Northern Nigerian Case Study," *Journal of Modern African Studies* 12 (March 1974): 57-67; Peter Waterman, "The 'Labor Aristocracy' in Africa: Introduction to a Debate," mimeographed (The Hague: Institute of Social Studies, n.d.); Peter Waterman, "Conservatism among Nigerian Workers: A Contribution to the Debate on Africa's 'Labour Aristocracy,' " mimeographed (The Hague: Institute of Social Studies, June 1974).

85. Interview in *Révolution Africaine*, 9 March 1963, cited in Woddis, *New Theories of Revolution*, p. 56.

86. Report to the Constitutive Congress of the PFA, 1 July 1959, cited in Woddis, *New Theories of Revolution*, p. 102.

87. Quoted in Woddis, *New Theories of Revolution*, p. 103.

88. G. Pfefferman, *Industrial Labour in Senegal* (New York: Praeger, 1968), p. 170.

89. For a story of how rural kinfolk are exploited in this way by their urban kinfolk, see Amu Djoleto, *The Strange Man* (London: Heinemann, 1967).

90. Ousmane Sembene, *God's Bits of Wood* (Garden City, N.Y.: Doubleday & Co., 1970).

91. *The Wretched of the Earth*, pp. 96-97.

92. Ibid., p. 89.

93. Ibid.

94. Ibid., p. 101.

95. Ibid.

96. Ibid.

97. Ibid., p. 110.

98. Ibid., p. 10.

99. Ibid., p. 98.

100. Ibid., p. 47.

101. Bakunin, *Works*, cd. Golos Truda, 4:212, quoted in Eugene Pyzuir, *The Doctrine of Anarchism of Michael A. Bakunin* (Chicago: Regnery, 1968), p. 75.

102. Mao Tse-Tung, "The Peasantry and Working Class Leadership," in Stuart R. Schram, *The Political Thought of Mao Tse-Tung* (New York: Praeger, 1969), p. 254.

103. Lin Piao, quoted in Y. Krasin, *The Dialectics of Revolutionary Process* (Moscow: Novosti Press Agency, 1972), p. 39.

104. *Revolution in the Revolution?*, p. 70.

105. Ibid., pp. 76-77.

106. *False Start in Africa*, p. 21.

107. "Critique of the Gotha Program," in Feuer, *Marx and Engels*, p. 125.

108. *The Wretched of the Earth*, p. 88.

109. Ibid.

110. Quoted in Woddis, *New Theories of Revolution*, p. 64. There is now a growing body of literature on the African peasantry. Some of the most im-

portant are: Szymon Chodak, "The Birth of an African Peasantry," *Canadian Journal of African Studies* 5 (1973): 327-47; L. A. Fallers, "Are African Cultivators to Be Called 'Peasants'?", *Current Anthropology* 2 (1961): 108-10; John Saul and Roger Woods, "African Peasantries," in Teodor Shanin, ed., *Peasants and Peasant Societies* (Harmondsworth, Middlesex: Penguin Books, 1971), pp. 103-14; Basil Davidson, "African Peasants and Revolution," *Journal of Peasant Studies* 1 (April 1974): 269-89; Colin Bundy, "The Emergence and Decline of a South African Peasantry," *African Affairs*, no. 285 (October 1972), pp. 369-88; Polly Hill, "The Myth of the Amorphous Peasantry: A Northern Nigerian Case Study," *Nigerian Journal of Economic and Social Studies* 10 (July 1968): 239-60; F. Mulambu-Mvuluya, "Introduction à l'étude du rôle des paysans dans les changements politiques," *Cahiers économiques et sociaux* 8 (September 1970): 435-50; Jacques J. Maquet, "La Participation de la classe paysanne au mouvement d'indépendance du Rwanda," *Cahiers d'études africaines* 4 (1964): 552-68.

111. Even in Guiné-Bissau it has been noticed that certain militants have shown reluctance to participate in armed units in regions other than their own; see Sheridan Johns, "Obstacles to Guerrilla Warfare: A South African Case Study," *Journal of Modern African Studies* 11 (June 1973): 302. See also Basil Davidson, *The Liberation of Guiné* (Harmondsworth, Middlesex: Penguin, 1969), pp. 102-3.

112. One is here reminded of the work of Daniel Lerner, *The Passing of Traditional Society* (New York: The Free Press, 1958), and Shanti Tangri, "Urbanization, Political Stability, and Economic Growth," in Jason L. Finkle and Richard W. Gable, eds., *Political Development and Social Change* (New York: John Wiley & Sons, 1968), pp. 305-19.

113. On certain aspects of peasant resistance in Ghana, see Dennis Austin, *Politics in Ghana: 1946-1960* (London: Oxford University Press, 1964); on peasant participation in Mau Mau, see Carl Rosberg, Jr., and John Nottingham, *The Myth of "Mau Mau": Nationalism in Kenya*; Donald Barnet and Karari Njama, *Mau Mau from Within*; Ladislav Venys, *A History of the Mau Mau Movement in Kenya* (Prague: Charles University Press, 1970); Frank Furedi, "The Social Composition of the Mau Movement in the White Highlands," *Journal of Peasant Studies* 1 (July 1974): 486-505.

114. Nguyen Nghe, "Frantz Fanon et les problèmes de l'indépendance," p. 28. "We have seen in Vietnam former soldiers of the Resistance return after nine years in the maquis to their opium-smoking; we have seen peasants who have been guerrillas for several years express fear of ghosts again because their political confidence in the party that used to direct them has been shaken as a result of the mistakes made in the course of agrarian reform."

115. Ibid., p. 29. "The peasant on his own can never have revolutionary consciousness; the militant from the cities should patiently detect the most gifted among the poor peasantry, educate them, and organize them; only after a long period of political work can the peasantry be mobilized."

116. David and Marina Ottaway, *Algeria: The Politics of a Socialist Revolution* (Berkeley and Los Angeles: University of California Press, 1970), p. 41.

117. Marie Perinbam, "Fanon and the Revolutionary Peasantry—the Algerian Case," *Journal of Modern African Studies* 11 (1973): 444.

118. *The Wretched of the Earth*, pp. 236–37.

119. Amilcar Cabral, *Revolution in Guinea* (New York: Monthly Review Press, 1966), p. 61.

120. *The Wretched of the Earth*, p. 109.

121. Robert Buijtenhuijs, *Le Mouvement "Mau Mau": une révolte paysanne et anti-coloniale en Afrique noire*, pp. 414–15, quoted in Perinbam, "Fanon and the Revolutionary Peasantry," p. 438.

122. *The Wretched of the Earth*, p. 114.

123. Ibid.

124. "Frantz Fanon et les problèmes de l'indépendance," p. 30. "With regard to the motivating force of the revolution, it consists of the working class, the peasant class, and the *petite bourgeoisie*. The leading role falls to the working class. The class of working peasants constitutes the main army of the revolution, the city bourgeoisie and the national bourgeoisie are the allies of the working class, yet with the difference that the national bourgeoisie is a conditional ally."

125. Ibid., p. 31. "The poor peasant may be a patriot and die heroically with a gun in his hand, but if he remains a peasant, he will be unable to lead a revolutionary movement. It is necessary to make a careful distinction between the motivating forces of the revolution and those that direct it. Throughout the history of peasant revolts, mere *jacqueries* always ended up in anarchy or to the advantage of feudal elements; never so far have the poor peasants been able to bring a revolution to fruition on their own."

126. Ibid. "For the revolution that should be taking place in the colonial countries at the present time is not only national; it should also be modern. This modern dimension cannot be conceived of by the peasantry; it can only be brought to the country by the bourgeoisie or the working class."

127. Woddis, *New Theories of Revolution*, pp. 57–58.

128. *The Wretched of the Earth*, p. 114.

129. Eric Wolf, "Peasant Rebellion and Revolution," in Norman Miller and Roderick Aya, eds., *National Liberation: Revolution in the Third World* (New York: Free Press, 1971), pp. 48–67; Eric Wolf, *Peasants* (Englewood Cliffs, N.J.: Prentice Hall, 1966), pp. 91–95; Eric Wolf, *Peasant Wars of the Twentieth Century* (London: Faber & Faber, 1971); Hamza Alavi, "Peasants and Revolution," *Socialist Register*, 1965, pp. 241–77. Another scholar who has also recently added his voice to the discussion is John Saul; see his illuminating article "African Peasants and Revolution," *Review of African Political Economy*, No. 1 (1974), pp. 41–68.

130. Fanon, *The Wretched of the Earth*, p. 103.

131. Ibid.

132. Ibid., pp. 102–3.

133. *Manifesto of the Communist Party*, in Feuer, *Marx and Engels*, p. 18.

134. Karl Marx and Fredrick Engels, *Selected Works* (Moscow: Progress Publishers, 1969), 1:219–20.

135. Ibid., 2:168.

136. Ibid., 1:220.

137. This refers to the incipient lumpen-proletariat; presumably, when it is well developed, it is no longer malleable.

138. Lenin, *Collected Works*, 2:216–23.

139. Mao Tse-Tung, *Analysis of the Classes in Chinese Society* (Peking: Foreign Languages Press, 1956), p. 11.

140. *The Wretched of the Earth*, p. 103.

141. Ibid.

142. Ibid., 102.

143. Ibid., p. 103.

144. Fred W. Riggs, *Administration in Developing Countries* (Boston: Houghton Mifflin, 1964), pp. 181–82.

145. *The Wretched of the Earth*, p. 109.

146. Ibid., p. 103.

147. Robin Cohen and David Michael, "The Revolutionary Potential of the African Lumpen proletariat: A Skeptical View," *Bulletin of the Institute of Development Studies* (Sussex), vol. 5 (1973), p. 34.

148. For a description of politics in Ghana during the period of nationalist agitation, see Dennis Austin, *Politics in Ghana*.

149. For details of this see G. O. Olusanya, "The Zikist Movement," *Journal of Modern African Studies* 4 (1966): 323–33.

150. Cohen and Michael, "The Revolutionary Potential of the African Lumpen-proletariat," p. 36.

151. Exceptions to this are: Christopher Allen, "'Lumpen-proletarians' and Revolution," in *Political Theory and Ideology in African Society* (Edinburgh: Centre for African Studies, 1970), pp. 91–115; Peter Worsley, "Frantz Fanon and the 'Lumpen proletariat,'" *Socialist Register*, 1972, pp. 193–230.

152. Peter Gutkind, "The Energy of Despair: Social Organization of the Unemployed in Two African Cities, Lagos and Nairobi," *Civilizations* 17 (1967): 194.

153. Basil Davidson, *The Liberation of Guiné*, pp. 50–51. There is a marked difference between the English rendering of the texts of Cabral's speeches and those that appeared in English under Cabral's own name in *Revolution in Guinea*, cited above.

154. "The Energy of Despair," p. 388.

155. Ibid., p. 385.

156. Fanon, *The Wretched of the Earth*, p. 103.

chapter six

fanon's vision of the ideal polity

. . . The choice of a socialist regime, a regime which is completely orientated towards the people as a whole and based on the principle that man is the most precious of all possessions will allow us to go forward more quickly and more harmoniously, and thus make impossible that caricature of society where all economic and political power is held in the hands of a few who regard the nation as a whole with scorn and contempt.

Frantz Fanon, *The Wretched of the Earth*

Let us try to create the whole man, whom Europe has been incapable of bringing to triumphant birth.

Ibid.

Writers on Frantz Fanon have concentrated more on the "negative" aspects of his writing, namely, his indictment of colonial rule with its culture of dependency, Western civilization, and his advocacy of revolutionary violence. Not much attention has been paid to his "positive" contributions—his suggestions for the creation of the kind of society in which the political ideals described in chapter 3 could be realized.

As we have seen in the previous chapters, the constraints on the emergence of the "authentic" man are alienation and oppressive social and political structures. Revolutionary violence cures alienation and destroys oppressive social and political structures. Our task here is to consider what, in the view of Fanon, are the nature and functioning of social and political arrangements that would enable man to express and to maintain his "authentic" existence. We shall also consider how such a society would function.

Like Marx, Fanon does not tell us how to construct the ideal society. Neither does he relate in any detailed manner the kinds of social and political structures that would obtain in such a society, nor in what precise way it would function. He provides a few general statements here and there as to the nature of the ideal society, its functioning, and the role that individuals and institutions would play in it. As with much of Fanon's writing, the accent is more on how society ought not to be organized and how it ought not to function.

fanon's socialist society

Notwithstanding the imprecise nature of Fanon's writing, he is clear about the type of society he has in mind: it is a non-repressive, non-authoritarian society; a society where men treat each other as ends and not as means to other ends; a society where men have meaningful relations with each other; in short, a society where there is no alienation. Fanon sees a socialist society as providing for this kind of ideal. For him such a society is not only possible but necessary for the underdeveloped countries if they are to avoid the mistakes of the Western industralized countries and attain "authentic" human existence. In Fanon's view the authoritarianism and the bureaucratic socialism of the Eastern European countries are to be deprecated as much as the capitalist class oppression of Western European countries. The true end of society is the liberation of man and the expression of his "authentic" existence, and socialism provides the social and political arrangements by which this can be attained.

What then is Fanon's socialist society? Fanon does not provide any detailed description of the socialist society he has in mind. He only presents fragments here and there. We shall therefore try to piece together the fragments and see whether a clear picture emerges.

Fanon claims that the first thing to do in the creation of such a society is to nationalize the means of production, distribution, and exchange. This is even more important in the underdeveloped countries, since the means of production are always owned by foreigners. Because of this, profits are constantly being returned to the "mother" country, instead of being reinvested in the country to furnish domestic capital to provide for economic development. Furthermore, the underdeveloped countries are kept in the position of producers of raw materials, and no infrastructure for an industrial society is built. It is necessary to nationalize the economy and to transform the whole structure of production in such a way as to achieve a self-sustained economic growth. In addition to effecting fundamental changes in the productive patterns and terminating the colonial dependency, nationalization also ensures a more equitable distribution of economic goods and resources. However, since in most of the underdeveloped countries the intermediary sectors of the economy[1] are also in the hands of foreigners, nationalization sometimes tends to be seen as the process of turning over this particular sector as well to the natives, who then enjoy the privileges formerly reserved for the colonialists. Fanon shows a keen awareness of this problem and counsels against its dangers:

> If the government wants to bring the country out of its stagnation and set it well on the road towards development and progress, it must first and foremost nationalize the middleman's trading sector. . . . In a colonial economy the intermediary sector is by far the most important. If you want to progress, you must decide in the first few hours to nationalize this sector.[2]

Another reason that Fanon advocates the nationalization of this sector is to prevent the national bourgeoisie from taking hold of it and using it as a base to entrench itself.

> The bourgeoisie, who wish to see both the triumph of the spirit of money-making and the enjoyment of consumer goods, and at the same time the triumph of their contemptuous attitude towards the mass of the people and the scandalous aspect of profit-making (should we not rather call it robbery?), in fact invests largely in this sector. The intermediary market which formerly was dominated by the settlers will be invaded by the young national bourgeoisie.[3]

The bourgeoisie invests in this sector in order to take hold of it and transfer into its own hands the privileges formerly enjoyed by the Europeans, to exploit the people in the same way that the colonialists did.[4]

It must be understood that for Fanon, just as nationalization does not mean native ownership of the intermediary sector of the economy, equally it does not mean bureaucratic control of the economy but rather its reorganization under the control of co-operatives.

> But it is clear that such a nationalization ought not to take on a rigidly state-controlled aspect. It is not a question of placing at the head of these services citizens who have had no political education. Every time such a procedure has been adopted it has been seen that the government has in fact contributed to the triumph of a dictatorship of civil servants who had been set in the

> mould of the former mother country, and who quickly showed themselves incapable of thinking in terms of the nation as a whole. These civil servants very soon began to sabotage the national economy and to throw its structure out of joint; under them, corruption, prevarication, the diversion of stocks and the black market came to stay. Nationalizing the intermediary sector means organizing wholesale and retail cooperatives on a democratic basis; it also means decentralizing these cooperatives by getting the mass of the people interested in the ordering of public affairs.[5]

Here we see a number of reasons why Fanon thinks that nationalization of the economy should not merely take the form of state control. In the first place, the civil servants lack political education; their minds are cast in the mold of the ideas and organizational patterns of the colonial regime. This predisposes to authoritarian controls, and is unsuitable for a regime the purpose of which is to attain the freedom of the individual. They are also corrupt. But perhaps the most important reason for advocating an economy along cooperative lines is that it allows the people to decide for themselves in what way to run the organization in order to provide maximum benefit for the nation. This would only work if the people and the nation have identity of interests. Fanon assumes this. It should be noted that Fanon assumes that the people would manage their co-operatives well and in the national interest. His basis for this is his belief that the people, but not the civil servants, have revolutionary consciousness. His argument assumes that the civil servants will always be corrupt and will always have "alienated consciousness." It is quite possible that after they have acquired revolutionary consciousness they could manage the nationalized economy efficiently and in the national interest. Fanon would object to this, since it robs the people of the chance to make their own decisions and put their destiny into their own hands.

Although Fanon was unequivocal in his preference for a socialist society, his concrete recommendations as far as nationalization is concerned seem to be limited to the intermediary sector. It has to be conceded, however, that he says that this is the first step, presumably to be followed by other steps that will nationalize the other sectors. The problem of the repatriation of profits and putting the economic destiny of the country into the hands of the people themselves would not be solved if only the intermediary sector of the economy were nationalized.

agrarian reform

In restructuring the economies of the underdeveloped countries, agrarian reforms deserve a very important consideration. In areas where peasants have mortgaged their lands to landlords who keep them in perpetual debt in order to reap the benefits of their labor, production is not only affected in the sense that one cannot expect the peasant to do his best in this condition of semi-slave labor, but this atmosphere of continuous exploitation breeds cynicism. "The people come to understand that wealth is not the fruit of labour but the result of organized, protected robbery."[6] Admittedly, this is not the situation all over Africa. Although in some places the peasants own their own lands, hired peasant labor is not uncommon, especially in areas of large European settlements where land alienation has created a class of landless peasantry. In all cases Fanon advocates land redistribution. He does not give details of how such redistribution is to be carried on, but he envisages a situation in which there will be no landlords and the land will belong to those who till it.[7] He does not talk of nationalization of land or even of agricultural cooperatives, either for production or for marketing. He contends that if the peasants are made to feel that they are working for themselves, and if they are shown how their work relates to the total productive capacity of the nation, it will bring out the best in them, and they will apply more responsibility and conscientiousness to their work. He paints a glowing picture of dramatic changes that have taken place in areas where such experiments have been put into operation.

> In those districts where we have been able to carry out successfully these interesting experiments, where we have watched man being created by revolutionary beginnings, the peasants have very clearly caught hold of the idea that the more intelligence you bring to your work, the more pleasure you will have in it. We have been able to make the masses understand that work is not simply the output of energy, nor the functioning of certain muscles, but that people work more by using their brains and their hearts than with only their muscles and their sweat.[8]

It is possible that people could work in the short run on such revolutionary élan. It is, however, difficult to expect peasants to work permanently on such a basis. But we have to remember that Fanon is talking not of any peasant but peasants whose lives and interests are entirely integrated with that of the nation. They do not see themselves as having interests different from those of the nation. This is the assumption underlying Fanon's argument all the time. The problem is whether it is possible to achieve such a close identity of interests. He has not told us anything about human nature to make us think that this is possible. Moreover, a peasant who achieves such a state of identification with the nation, loses his individuality, which is what Fanon wants him to express. Fanon does not say anything about the relationship between the cooperative and the state. Are the cooperatives completely independent of state authority or are they to enjoy some measure of autonomy? If they are to be completely autonomous, how is one to coordinate their activities in such a way as to run them economically and efficiently? If they are to be allowed limited authority, what is the precise limitation, and who is to have the final say? How does one fight bureaucratization in this case? These are details that Fanon does not consider. Like Marx, he presents his vision and leaves the details to future generations to work out.

the political system

I have already indicated the economic features of the social system that Fanon envisaged. Here we shall deal with the political features of the system. The discussion will center around the party system and the administrative structure.

The party system. Fanon assumes that in his ideal society there will be a single-party system. Although he delivers some of his most virulent strictures against the single-party system, it should be remembered that his attack is not on the system as such but on the way it has been functioning in Africa.

The single party should be a revolutionary party, organized not only in the big urban centers but also in the rural areas. In fact, rural organization is even more important if it is remembered that it is in the rural areas that the peasants live, and the peasants, according to Fanon, are the most revolutionary. He suggests that the rural organization of the party should be done without destroying the traditional leaders or the traditional structures. Instead they should be made to assume "progressive" roles in the new society.

> The political parties do not manage to organize the country districts. Instead of using existing structures and giving them a nationalist or progressive character, they mean to try and destroy living tradition in the colonial framework. . . . Thus from the capital city they will "parachute" organizers into the villages who are either unknown or too young, and who, armed with instructions from the central authority, mean to treat the *douar* or village like a factory cell.

> The traditional chiefs are ignored, sometimes even persecuted. The makers of the future nation's history trample unconcernedly over small local disputes, that is to say the only existing national events, whereas they ought to make of village history—the history of traditional conflicts between clans and tribes—a harmonious whole, at one with the decisive action to which they call on the people to contribute.[9]

Fanon seems to think that the traditional structures will be maintained, or only slightly modified. It is difficult, however, to imagine how this could be done within the framework of the socialist society he envisages. Most of the traditional structures in Africa are feudal in nature. The main feature of a feudal society is the hierarchical system of authority and recruitment, based largely on ascriptive criteria.

It is difficult to see how this can be reconciled with the egalitarianism of a socialist society. One can understand that caution should be taken in dealing with traditional rulers and that it is strategically unwise to provoke them. On the other hand, considering the depth and rapidity of the changes that Fanon advocates, it is unlikely that traditional institutions could be used to accomplish them. He writes: "Without any period of transition, there is a total, complete and absolute substitution."[10] Traditional institutions can be used to effect changes within the traditional structure, but when the change desired is the structure itself, and of such a nature as the above quotation implies, such a method is unlikely to yield lasting results.

Besides, as Fanon strongly argues, political structures do determine political behavior. This is the main reason that colonial structures should be, not reformed, but completely destroyed. But if traditional structures can be given a "nationalist" and "progressive character," why can we not do the same with colonial structures? The reason is that the traditional structures in the colonial society are not like the ones in the pre-colonial society. They have been adapted in such a way as to function to the advantage of the colonial regime, so that in a way they are not different from the colonial administrative and political structure itself.

Traditional rulers have also reaped some of the benefits of colonial rule, which provided them new avenues for acquiring wealth. Their position vis-à-vis their people was considerably strengthened. A ruler could do practically whatever he wanted so long as he remained in the good graces of the colonial rulers. Traditional sanctions on their power and authority did not have much hold. In a way, then, the traditional rulers, like the urban petite bourgeoisie and the national bourgeoisie, are among the privileged members of the colonial system. If Fanon denounces the urban petite bourgeoisie and the national bourgeoisie for reaping the benefits of colonial rule, which makes them uninterested in authentic decolonization, why does he think that traditional rulers could be persuaded to serve an effective party organization at the grass-roots level, a move that would eventually dispossess them of their power and influence?[11]

In one passage Fanon claims that the urban militant is immediately welcome and given protection by the peasant:

> They [the urban militants] fall back towards the countryside and the mountains, towards the peasant people. From the beginning, the peasantry closes in around them, and protects them. . . . The peasant's cloak will wrap him around with a gentleness and firmness that he never suspected.[12]

Yet, talking about the organizers of the nationalist parties, he tells us that the organizers from the capitals are "unknown" and "young." Presumably this is a disadvantage to them. But why does the fact that the urban organizers are unknown and young arouse the suspicion of the peasants, whereas in the case of the urban militants this does not seem to make any difference?

What accounts for the differences between the treatment of the urban organizers and the urban militants? Is there any perceptible difference between the two as far as the peasant is concerned, particularly on initial contact?

Another point that Fanon makes concerns decentralization of the party:

> In an under-developed country, the leading members of the party ought to avoid the capital as if it had the plague. They ought, with some few exceptions, to live in the country districts. The centralization of all activity in the city ought to be avoided. No excuse of administrative discipline should be taken as legitimizing that excrescence of a capital which is already over-populated and over-developed with regard to nine-tenths of the country. The party should be decentralized in the extreme. It is the only way to bring life to regions which are dead, those regions which are not yet awakened to life.[13]

Fanon goes on to suggest that there should be at least one member of the political bureau in each district. He should not be the head, nor even hold any authority in the area. It will also be necessary to set up in the regions officials with full powers whose duty will be to facilitate the growth of political consciousness.[14] This decentralization of the party has a number of advantages. It prevents the center from becoming unnecessarily loaded with all forms of minor administrative decisions that could well be taken in the regions. Regional devolution of power gives a feeling of meaningful participation in the political process on the part of the people at the local level. This increases identification with the party and consequently heightens legitimacy. It also has the advantage of fostering a closer union and identity of interests between the rank and file and the party leadership, and prevents the kind of pathology in political parties that Robert Michels describes in his *Political Parties*. In this way the party does not become a mere apparatus for transmitting the orders of the leadership, but provides a two-way flow of information. The party becomes what it ought to be: "an organism through which they as a people exercise their authority and express their will."[15]

Another important aspect of the decentralization of the party is that it discourages rural-urban migration. The concentration of all offices and government departments in the capital gives it the image of a center of power and a place of endless possibilities. Rural dwellers are thus unnecessarily attracted to the capital. The psychological effect of having high party and government officials living in the districts and rural areas would be considerable. The effect also of having party leaders living in areas different from their areas of origin (as one would expect from Fanon's writings) would be in the long run to reduce feelings of ethnicity.

Fanon does not give us details of the decentralization of the party. What is to be the relationship between the party at the local level and at the national level? If the local branches are to have complete autonomy, as he seems to suggest, then we would have not a single party but a multiplicity of parties. How is one going to coordinate the activities of such a large number of autonomous groups? And how is one going to ensure ideological unity in such a case? Furthermore, such decentralization poses problems in the area of decision-making. In the modern world important decisions have to be made quickly. How can one refer all issues to the local branches for discussion, especially when we remember the way Fanon expects decisions to be arrived at, namely, by all the people collectively taking part. Besides, there are complex questions of foreign policy and foreign trade that could best be handled by experts, and no useful purpose would be served by sending them to the branches for discussion. Fanon, of course, assumes that the people have the ability to understand everything if it is properly explained to them.

The assumption underlying decentralization is that

the country people have not only the capacity but also the willingness to undertake the burden of decision-making and development. The claim has often been made that the country people or the masses as a whole lack understanding of the complex issues of politics, and are apathetic and passive. Fanon rejects this view:

> An isolated individual may obstinately refuse to understand a problem, but the group or the village understands with disconcerting rapidity.[16]

It is important to note the words "may obstinately refuse to understand." He does not say that the individual does not understand. He has the capacity to understand, but he may refuse, due to fear or suspicion. In the security of the group he lets down his guard. Hence the group understands with "disconcerting rapidity"—disconcerting, of course, to the urban intellectuals and the bureaucrats! It could be also that Fanon is here claiming that in a collectivity a common understanding develops that transcends the understanding of the particular individuals that compose the group. This collective understanding is the common will of the group. However, the use of the phrase "may obstinately refuse to understand" and the voluntaristic notion it implies make such an interpretation rather unlikely.

The intellectuals, politicians, and bureaucrats in the underdeveloped countries, in spite of the rhetoric of populism, have a low opinion of the country people and the masses generally, and sometimes treat them with disdain. They regard them in the same way as the colonial officials did: lazy, superstitious, apathetic, passive, and lacking in understanding of the issues and problems of politics. Fanon's contention is that it is not so much that the masses do not understand as that the intellectuals fail to communicate with them in such a way as to make themselves understood.

> It is true that if care is taken to use only a language that is understood by graduates in law and economics, you can easily prove that the masses have to be managed from above. But if you speak the language of every day; if you are not obsessed by the perverse desire to spread confusion and to rid yourself of the people, then you will realize that the masses are quick to seize every shade of meaning and to learn all the tricks of the trade. . . . Everything can be explained to the people, on the single condition that you really want them to understand.[17]

This profound faith in the ability of the people underlies much of Fanon's thinking and is the basis of his strategy for authentic decolonization and development.

Fanon insists on the separation of the party and the government. The party is the collective representation of the entire people. "The party is not a tool in the hands of the government. Quite on the contrary, the party is a tool in the hands of the people."[18] The government is the executive arm of the party.

> The less there is of confusion and duality of powers, the more the party will play its part of guide and the more surely it will constitute for the people a decisive guarantee. If the party is mingled with the government, the fact of being a party militant means that you take the short cut to gain private ends, to hold a post in the government, step up the ladder, get promotion and make a career for yourself.[19]

It is not clear here whether Fanon is arguing that party members should not hold positions in the government. If the government is to be the executive arm of the party and carry out its dictates, it is necessary that those who carry out these dictates be not only well acquainted with the goals and ideals of the party, but also have sympathy with them. At the minimum there should be a concordance of ideological interests between the government and the party. Without this, one cannot expect members of the government to carry out the dictates of the party with the devotion that the revolutionary socialism of

Fanon implies. Moreover, it is difficult, if not impossible, to make any meaningful separation between the party and the government in a single-party state. The whole logic of such a separation makes sense only in a two- or multi-party state. Fanon's suggestion to keep the two separate is motivated largely by the desire to prevent opportunists and careerists from using the party as a ladder for upward social mobility in the government. But maintaining a strict separation of the party and the government is not the way to deal with the problem, for an opportunist is a danger to the developmental efforts of the people and the ideals of the nation, whether he is in the party's bureau or in the government offices. Fanon does not provide a way to ensure an uncorrupted party membership.

What role does a party organized along the lines discussed above play in the lives of the people? In the first place, the party in this case is not a mechanism for electing public officials every few years, or an apparatus for transmitting orders from the leadership, but a "direct expression of the masses."[20] In Fanon's words:

> The party is not an administration responsible for transmitting government orders; it is the energetic spokesman and the incorruptible defender of the masses.[21]

This sounds very much like Rousseau. The party represents the general will (energetic spokesman) and always aims at the general good (incorruptible defender of the masses). The party, for Fanon, is both the general will and the community. The individual expresses his "true" being or his freedom when he is identified with the party and takes part in its deliberations and activities. The purpose of human existence is the expression of freedom. The duty of the leaders of the underdeveloped countries, therefore, is to fashion a party in such a way that it will allow man to express his freedom;

and for Fanon, a party organized along the lines discussed above meets that requirement.

However, for a party to play the above role effectively, it should be identified with the nation and the state. Fanon, however, insists on separation of the party and the state. Unless there is no separation between the party, nation, and state, each institution will develop its own interests that may conflict with the interests of the others.

the administrative structure

Like the political party, the administrative structure should be completely decentralized. One should avoid the separation of the town and the country, and the separation of the bureaucrats and the leaders from the lives and problems of the majority of the people in the country. Fanon writes:

> The native civil servants and technicians ought not to bury themselves in diagrams and statistics, but rather in the heart of the people. They ought not to bristle up every time there is a question of a move to be made to the "interior." We should no longer see the young women of the country threaten their husbands with divorce if they do not manage to avoid being appointed to a rural post.[22]

It may be argued that in Africa there is no need to stress the necessity of this intimate social contact between the urban intelligentsia (the senior civil servants, technicians, and so on) and the rural people, for the reason that, because of the claims of kinship, they already maintain intimate contact with the rural people and are aware of their problems. This situation is true only to a very limited extent. In the first place, most of those who end up as top civil servants and technicians hail from the urban and not the rural areas.[23] Second, the few who come from the rural areas are so concerned with trying to escape what they regard as the ugly disabilities of rural life (lack of social amenities and such) and their obligations to their kin groups that they try to minimize their contacts with the rural area. Besides, the colonial practice of sending civil servants there as a form of punishment has not helped to erase this antipathy. Such intimate contacts with the rural areas as Fanon advocates help the bureaucrat to acquire firsthand knowledge of the rural area, which is necessary for the kinds of crucial decisions he makes. Further, it has the effect of making the rural people view the government officials as one of them, and this eventually helps to increase the government's legitimacy.

Fanon further suggests regional devolution of power and decision-making, and a system of rotating capitals. This has the effect of involving the rural masses in the process of development, preventing uneven development, and minimizing rural-urban migration.

There are some who will look askance at the idea of rotating capitals. Far from dispersing limited resources and making the building of infrastructure difficult, it will lead to an even development of infrastructure and a sense of greater personal commitment on the part of the people toward the government. After all, the idea of rotating capitals is not new. It was practiced in medieval Europe, and it was one method that medieval monarchs used to make their rule effective in all areas of the land. In the underdeveloped countries it could be employed to integrate all sections of the country into a single community.

model of decision-making

The kind of political structure envisaged is one that will enable the mass of the people to participate effectively, not only in political deliberations, but also in the political process itself. In this the leaders are expected to play the role of guiding the people in their decisions. They must not on any account impose their own decisions on the people. After decisions have been reached, they are to articulate and express the will of the people. Fanon's vision is that of a society where the people hold the primacy of power. It is an intensely populist regime. To underline the importance of the involvement of the people in the decision-making and in the running of the society, he writes:

> In an under-developed country, experience proves that the important thing is not that three hundred people form a plan and decide upon carrying it out, but that the whole people plan and decide even if it takes them twice or three times as long.[24]

This insistence on the involvement of the people, as I have already indicated above, is premised on a deep faith in the capacity of the people to make rational decisions and to be able to determine their interests.

In Fanon's polity the individual is completely identified with the society. Like Rousseau and Plato, he makes no distinction between a good person and a good citizen.

> To educate the masses politically is to make the totality of the nation a reality to each citizen. It is to make the history of the nation part of the personal experience of each of its citizens.[25]

Continuing the same theme of the link between the individual and the nation, he writes:

> Individual experience, because it is national and because it is a link in the chain of national existence, ceases to be individual, limited and shrunken and is enabled to open out into the truth of the nation and of the world.[26]

The implications of this are clear. If the individual is as closely identified with the community as Fanon suggests here, he is unlikely to develop interests antagonistic to, or even different from, those of the community.

Hence, conflicts between the individual and the society will be completely unknown. In fact, it is even doubtful whether there would be interpersonal conflicts in such a society. Fanon's emphasis on the whole people collectively taking part in decision-making suggests that he is thinking of direct democracy. It is significant to note that he does not say anything about representative institutions either at the local or national level. It is in this sense that one can appreciate his argument for radical decentralization. It seems, however, that the one possible effect of radical decentralization, coupled with total identification of the individual with the community, would be to encourage localism and create in the long run not one community but a series of communities, unless there is a deep and pervasive ideological consensus in the entire nation. Although Fanon does not specifically state it, he seems to assume such a state of affairs. Fanon also seems to disregard the question of ethnicity. The experience of the Soviet Union and East European countries should warn us that the resilience and the claims of ethnicity cannot be so easily ignored.

the place of art, culture, the press, and the army in the ideal society

In Fanon's ideal society, art and culture will not be for entertainment only. The concept of art for art's sake will have no place. Art will be didactic and it will aim at promoting the ends of society.

> The colonized man who writes for his people ought to use the past with the intention of opening the future, as an invitation to action and a basis for hope.[27]

This should also be the role of other branches of learning like history, literature, painting, and so on.

In Fanon's conception the role of the press, too, is subordinated to the goals of the society. The press is not free to provide just any kind of information, but only that which helps the people to arrive at the goals they have set for themselves. Thus, in the underdeveloped countries, it is more useful to know of Cuba's efforts to increase sugar production or of Burma's efforts to combat illiteracy than to know of the scandals of the Italian aristocracy.[28] The questions that are always asked with regard to such a line of reasoning are these: Who is to decide what precise information helps the people to arrive at the goals they have set for themselves? Is it possible that there could be a conflict of opinion as to what constitutes the "right" information? Fanon does not confront such problems. It has to be noted, however, that if a society is fashioned on the lines he suggests, with such depth and pervasiveness of ideological consensus and such close identification of the individual with the nation, and such radical decentralization and meaningful participation in decision-making as his vision conjures, such problems would not assume significance as to deserve much attention and are not likely to cause conflict. There might be only procedural differences but not fundamental differences as to end in conflict. Of course, whether it would be possible to achieve this complete fusion of the individual with the nation is another matter.

Fanon makes the same arguments with respect to the army. It provides labor for public works and becomes an agent of development. The military is not only a school of war, it is a school of civic and political education. It is completely politicized and shows the same level of commitment to the society as do the civilians. Politicization of the army is necessary to overcome the "colonial mentality" of most of Africa's armies and to replace it with the concept of a soldier as a good citizen who happens to play the role of defending the nation. This can best be done by raising a people's militia, thus avoiding the costs of keeping a large standing army, and preventing the formation of a military caste. If all the people are to participate in decision-making and in developing the country, then the task of defending the country need not fall exclusively on the shoulders of a select group of people. It should be the responsibility of the entire nation. Failure to do this has led to disastrous consequences. With an uncanny insight Fanon wrote in 1961:

> Care must be taken to avoid turning the army into an autonomous body which sooner or later, finding itself idle and without any definite mission, will "go into politics" and threaten the government. Drawing-room generals, by dint of haunting the corridors of government departments, come to dream of manifestoes. The only way to avoid this menace is to educate the army politically, in other words to nationalize it.[29]

In addition to suggesting the way by which alienation is overcome and freedom gained, i.e., through revolutionary violence, Fanon also suggests the social and political arrangements that will enable man to express and to maintain his freedom. He sees these social and political arrangements as a society where the economy is nationalized and managed on a cooperative basis by the people themselves. The political arrangements of the society are also such that the people take effective part not only in the decision-making process but also in the actual political process. Through participation in the political process, the individual rediscovers his sense of community in the society and becomes completely integrated with it. Although the political structures and the institutions of the new society are not exactly the same as in the pre-colonial society, the political and social arrangements are such that they function to make man express the fullness of his nature, in the same way as the pre-colonial societies did. In the new society alienation is completely overcome, and man lives his full and "authentic" existence. Man recovers his innocence lost during the colonial interlude.

I have raised a number of questions and pointed out the inadequacies of such a society. Fanon is vague in his delineation of the features of his ideal polity. In delineating the economic features, he mentions, as a first step, the nationalization of the intermediary sectors of the economy and the organization of cooperatives. We are not given details of the subsequent steps to be taken to get the processes of production, distribution, and exchange nationalized, as his revolutionary socialism implies. His political and administrative decentralization poses problems of decision-making and coordination, and his idea of the complete identification of the individual with the society could take away from the person the individuality he so ardently desires for man. He does not say anything about representative institutions, and it is difficult to imagine how one can construct a modern society on the basis of direct democracy. He says nothing about force, coercion, or the settlement of disputes. Presumably, he does not expect any conflicts in a society of this sort, yet he has a place for the army, which must be meant then for an external enemy. We may raise many more questions about Fanon, but let us remember that he wrote with the impatience of a revolutionary fighting against an oppressive social order. In spite of the fragmentary nature of his writing, his arguments demonstrate the use of creative imagination to tackle the central problem of human existence: how to overcome the duality of man and his environment. The Christian and Hindu philosophers saw the answer in man's complete surrender to God. Fanon, like Plato, Rousseau, Hegel, and Marx before him, saw the answer in man's complete absorption in community, or, as Hegel would say, in the social substance.

1. This usually refers to retail trade and service enterprises.
2. *The Wretched of the Earth*, p. 144.
3. Ibid.

4. For the economic manipulations of this class in Ghana, see Fitch and Oppenheimer, *Ghana: End of an Illusion*, pp. 66-80.

5. *The Wretched of the Earth*, pp. 144-45.

6. Ibid., p. 154.

7. Ibid.

8. Ibid.

9. Ibid., pp. 89-90.

10. Ibid., p. 27.

11. Amilcar Cabral reportedly told Basil Davidson that one of the most serious problems encountered by the revolution in Guiné was the hostility of the Fula chiefs; see Davidson, *The Liberation of Guiné*, p. 60.

12. *The Wretched of the Earth*, p. 100.

13. Ibid., p. 149.

14. Ibid., p. 150.

15. Ibid., p. 149.

16. Ibid., p. 152.

17. Ibid.

18. Ibid., p. 149.

19. Ibid.

20. Ibid., p. 151.

21. Ibid.

22. Ibid.

23. Margaret Peil, for example, argues that in Ghana the best degrees, and consequently the best jobs, go to students with early advantage, those born in cities of over 40,000 and who attend elite secondary schools and enter the university right from the sixth form; see "The Ghanaian University Students: The Broadening Base," *British Journal of Sociology* 16 (1965): 19-28. David Finlay found that of a sample of Legon students interviewed in 1966, 69.4 percent came from urban areas, whereas only 23.1 percent of the country's population was urban; see "Students and Politics in Ghana," *Daedalus* 97 (Winter 1968): 53.

24. *The Wretched of the Earth*, pp. 155-56.

25. Ibid., p. 161.

26. Ibid.

27. Ibid., p. 187.

28. Ibid., p. 164.

29. Ibid., p. 163.

chapter seven

conclusion

I argued in the introduction that there are several perspectives from which one can approach Fanon, none of which by itself yields a clear understanding of the totality and complexity of his thought. Fanon can be studied from the point of view of political biography, or political philosophy, or social science, or an action-oriented program, or as utopia. To do justice to his writings, it is necessary to consider his ideas from all these points of view; and in the preceding pages, I have tried to evaluate Fanon's thought paying close attention to all these dimensions.

political biography

The perspective of political biography yields an image of Fanon as a man of considerable intellectual stature, sensitivity, perception, restlessness, and impatience. All these are reflected in his writings. Fanon was a man of thought, but also a man of action who committed himself to the course of human freedom. He was deeply committed to praxis, and in his writings one notices how frequently he alternates from description to prescription. He was personally preoccupied with recognition, a preoccupation that plagued him all his life. Thus as the darkest child of an upper-middle-class family in a socioeconomic setting where color played an important role, he was concerned with recognition. As a black intellectual in France, in an environment where color took precedence over achievement, he was also preoccupied with recognition. In North Africa he was also concerned with recognition in a situation where race, religion, and nationality were put above everything else. I am not arguing here that Fanon's ideas arose out of his private concern with recognition, but it is important to understand the social context in which he grew up and matured in order to appreciate the fullness of his thought. The biographical approach provides us, as we have seen in the preceding pages, with an insight into the personality and mind of the individual we are dealing with. And for a man whose ideas were so intricately linked with his life, this is important if we are to understand him fully.

political philosophy

Fanon presents us with a state of human unfreedom, a program of action to end such a situation, and a vision of life in freedom. Fanon's life, actions, and ideas are all premised on the idea of freedom. His commitment to praxis, however, discourages linguistic analysis or intellectual conceptualization. Thus, although freedom was his chief concern, he does not philosophize on the nature of freedom. He was more interested in bringing freedom into being. In spite of this, his writing is premised on the philosophical assumption that freedom is the supreme destiny of man. He even goes on to define man in terms of freedom. That is, man is only man when he is free, and Fanon insists on total freedom. This insistence, however, creates certain problems. If it is claimed that man has an essential nature, which, according to Fanon, is his incessant quest for freedom, then his freedom is limited by this essential nature, i.e., his *quest* for freedom; and in that case one cannot insist on the totality of human freedom. Insistence on total freedom also leads to philosophical anarchism, and one does discern some anarchic trends in Fanon's writings. Fanon, however, avoids such a conclusion, and instead recommends a society based on a fusion of Rousseau's ideal community and Marx's communistic ideal.

Although Fanon abandons his insistence on the existentialist notion of total freedom in his later works and accepts the influence of past history and the socioeconomic environment on the individual, he still regards social change as brought about through willful and determinate actions of men.

There are other philosophical dimensions of Fanon's thinking, but since they do not relate directly to the theme of freedom, I have not found it necessary to discuss them here.

social science

Fanon's work could also be regarded as a work of social science. In this regard he is concerned with examining the nature of the obstacles to human freedom. He uses his knowledge of history, sociology, psychology, and philosophy to discern and comment on the nature of these obstacles.

He identifies the principal obstacle to human freedom as alienation. His study in this sphere is based on his observations in Martinique and France, and his psychiatric experience in Algeria. He discusses the origins, the nature, and the manifestations of alienation, both in the dependent countries and in the independent countries of Africa. He also discusses the mechanisms that produce alienation in the colonial setting. Here he operates like a physician. He probes to find the root cause of the "disease" and works out a diagnosis before coming up with a prescription. He deals with human society as a doctor deals with a patient. He stratifies African society, and examines the revolutionary potential of each class. It is perhaps to Fanon's credit that class analysis is being increasingly employed by "respectable" social scientists in the analysis of the pattern and structure of African politics.[1]

action-oriented program

I have also stated that for Fanon analysis is useful only as a prelude to action. His analysis of the social situation in the underdeveloped countries therefore culminates in his drawing up a blueprint for revolutionary action. He prescribes revolutionary violence as the way to end alienation. Violence frees alienated consciousness and destroys social and political institutions that inhibit man from maintaining and expressing his freedom. His advocacy of violence is premised on the view that alienation is caused by the violence of the colonial regime. This violence sets in motion a chain of dialectical changes that can only be resolved by a recourse to violence on the part of the native in order to achieve his freedom. Fanon, as we have already pointed out, is not as unequivocal in his advocacy of violence for the emancipation of alienated consciousness as some of his interpreters would have us believe. He concedes that on one level it is possible to achieve liberation of consciousness through political education provided by the party. On the other hand, the work of breaking down the social and political institutions of the colonial society can only be achieved through violence. However, once it is conceded that it is possible to achieve liberation of consciousness through nonviolent means, the argument for the necessity of violence to break the social and political institutions of the colonial state loses some of its force.

utopia

The utopian dimension of Fanon's work is concerned with the construction of the ideal society. As I have already stated, his philosophical assumptions lead him to construct an ideal society that is a mixture of Marxian socialism and Rousseau's ideal community. The economic organization of Fanon's ideal society is Marxian, and the political organization is Rousseauistic. Fanon, however, does not share the same distrust of the people that we see in Rousseau's work; hence, he does not install any legislator over them. In Fanon's ideal society it is difficult to imagine what role the leaders are supposed to play, apart from political education, since he insists that all the people collectively should take part in decision-making.

Taking all these dimensions of Fanon's thought into consideration, we see that his ideas form a coherent body of thought on freedom and how it can be attained by the oppressed of the underdeveloped countries. Admittedly, other writers have dealt with some of the specific problems of oppressed people in the Third World; but what is significant about Fanon is that he not only deals with the totality of the problems within a framework that is analytically meaningful, and that commands intellectual attention, but he also raises his recommendations to the level of a general theory of social action.

To say this is, of course, not to deny that there are weaknesses in Fanon's analyses. Not even the most sympathetic critic would fail to notice the inconsistencies, contradictions, questionable premises, conclusions that do not follow from the evidence provided, and many more. These have been discussed at length in the preceding pages, and there is no need to restate them here. The important question is to consider the policy implications of Fanon's ideas. What do we learn from Fanon, and where do we go from here?

Just as Fanon argues that it is foolish for the national bourgeoisie of the underdeveloped countries to apply mechanically what they have learned in European universities to the underdeveloped countries, in the same way it would be foolish of us to try to apply Fanon's ideas without any modification.

The generality of his pronouncements calls for modifications before they are applied to specific situations. Thus, it would be wrong to seek to apply Fanon's theory of revolutionary war to the African condition, or for that matter to any condition, without any modification to suit the specific local conditions. In Africa alone we have to take into consideration the peculiar socioeconomic environment. Hence, we have to evolve one strategy for the countries that have gained political independence, and another strategy for the countries that are still under foreign domination. We also have to take into consideration the internal social structure. Societies like South Africa, with their multiracial compositions, need a different strategy from racially homogeneous societies like Guiné-Bissau. Even among the countries that have gained political independence, revolutionary strategy would dictate different techniques depending on the internal objective conditions. Thus, in places like Ghana and Nigeria, where a more developed and politically conscious urban proletariat exists, it would be bad politics to write them off completely because Fanon says to do so. The urban working class in such situations, because of its size and its strategic role in the economy, should be seriously taken into account. If it is given revolutionary direction, it could play a useful role in the revolutionary movement. Considering that in many of the underdeveloped countries, because of the problem of uneven development, the urban centers represent the centers of power, the demonstration effect of the action of the urban working class in the cities would be very important. When it is aligned with the poor peasantry and the revolutionary intellectuals, the chances of building an effective revolutionary movement would be greatly enhanced. One must also not forget the armies. Considering the significant role they play in the politics of Latin America, the Middle East, Asia, and are beginning to play in Africa, it would be foolish to ignore them. An attempt should be made to win over the army to the side of the revolutionary movement, or at least to ensure its neutrality. After the revolution, steps should be taken immediately to politicize it. The universities and colleges also should not be isolated from the currents of revolutionary thought. The idealism of the youth should be utilized and channeled to the service of the revolution, so that it becomes the intellectual forerunner of the revolutionary movement.

Furthermore, one cannot leave the urban areas completely, nor should every guerrilla action start in the rural areas. The role of the Tupamaros in Uruguay is quite effective,[2] and if this action was coordinated with a rural uprising, it would be difficult to put down. It is necessary to combine rural mobilization with urban politicization. The importance of the urban centers is underlined by the fact that, although the PAIGC now controls about two-thirds of the land in Guiné-Bissau, it has still not succeeded in dislodging the Portuguese, who have erected barricades for themselves in the urban areas. Unless the PAIGC guerrillas carry the war into the urban areas and sow panic among the urban residents, the outcome of the war will remain undecided.[3] The enemy must be made to realize that no part of the country is safe for him.

In countries like Tanzania, where both the national

bourgeoisie and the urban proletariat are small and weak, the role of the peasantry naturally takes on added significance, and this has to be taken into consideration in planning revolutionary strategy.

It is important to remember that revolutionary theory and action should be rooted in the specific socioeconomic realities of each country.

Thus there is a lot we can learn from Fanon, but only if we make use of his ideas imaginatively and flexibly, making necessary modifications here and there to suit particular situations, in the same way that Mao made use of Marx and Lenin. It is only in this way that we shall derive much benefit from Fanon's work, and not by assigning to it the status of infallible scripture to be applied mechanically to all situations.

1. See Michael Lofchie, "The Uganda Coup: Class Action by the Military," *Journal of Modern African Studies* 10 (May 1972): 19–35; Ali A. Mazrui, "The Lumpen Proletariat and the Lumpen Militariat: African Soldiers as a New Political Class," *Political Studies* 21 (March 1973): 1–12; Gavin Williams, "The Social Stratification of a Neo-Colonial Economy: Western Nigeria," in Christopher Allen and R. W. Johnson, eds., *African Perspectives* (Cambridge: At the University Press, 1970), pp. 225–50.

2. For information on the Tupamaros see Alain Labrousse, *The Tupamaros*, trans. Dinah Livingstone (Harmondsworth, Middlesex: Penguin Books, 1973)

3. This was written before the coup that toppled the Caetano regime in April 1974 and that led to the withdrawal of Portuguese armed forces from Guiné-Bissau and, consequently, the recognition of Guiné-Bissau's independence.

bibliography

Books by Frantz Fanon

L'An V de la révolution algérienne. Paris: François Maspéro, 1959.

Black Skin, White Masks. Translated by Charles L. Markmann. New York: Grove Press, Evergreen Books, 1967.

Les Damnés de la terre. Paris: François Maspéro, 1961.

A Dying Colonialism. Translated by Haakon Chevalier. New York: Grove Press, Evergreen Books, 1967.

Peau noir, masques blancs. Paris: Editions du Seuil, 1952.

Pour la révolution africaine. Paris: François Maspéro, 1964.

Toward the African Revolution. Translated by Haakon Chevalier. New York: Grove Press, Evergreen Books, 1969.

The Wretched of the Earth. Translated by Constance Farrington. Harmondsworth, Middlesex: Penguin, 1967.

Select Bibliography

BOOKS

ACHEBE, CHINUA. *A Man of the People.* London: Heinemann, 1966.

ADLER, ALFRED. *Understanding Human Nature.* New York: Fawcett, 1954.

AGEL, JEROME. *The Radical Therapist.* New York: Ballantine Books 1971.

ALLEN, ROBERT L. *Black Awakening in Capitalist America.* New York: Doubleday, 1969

ALROY, GIL CARL. *The Involvement of Peasants in Internal Wars.* Princeton, N.J.: Center of International Studies, Princeton University, 1966.

ARENDT, HANNAH. *On Revolution.* New York: Viking Press, 1965.

———. *On Violence.* New York: Harcourt Brace & World, 1969.

BARBER, BENJAMIN R. *Superman and Common Men.* New York: Praeger, 1971.

BARNETT, DONALD, and KARARI NJAMA. *Mau Mau from Within.* London: Macgibbon and Kee, 1966.

BAY, CHRISTIAN. *The Structure of Freedom.* New York: Atheneum, 1968.

BETTS, RAYMOND F. *Assimilation and Association in French Colonial Theory.* New York: Columbia University Press, 1961.

BLAUNER, ROBERT. *Alienation and Freedom.* Chicago: University of Chicago Press, 1964.

BOUVIER, PIERRE. *Fanon.* Paris: Editions Universitaires, 1971.

BRACE, RICHARD, and JOAN BRACE. *Algerian Voices.* Princeton, N.J.: Van Nostrand, 1965.

BRECHER, MICHAEL. *Nehru: A Political Biography.* London: Oxford University Press, 1959.

BUIJTENHUIJS, ROBERT. *Le Mouvement "Mau Mau": une rĕvolte paysanne et anti-coloniale en Afrique Noire.* The Hague, 1971.

CABRAL, AMILCAR. *National Liberation and Culture.* Syracuse, N.Y.: Program of Eastern African Studies, Syracuse University, Occasional Paper No. 57, 1970.

———. *Revolution in Guinea.* New York: Monthly Review Press, 1969.

CALVERT, PETER. *Revolution.* London: Pall Mall, 1970.

CAMUS, ALBERT. *The Rebel.* New York: Random House, Vintage Books, 1956.

CARMICHAEL, STOKELEY, and CHARLES HAMILTON. *Black Power.* New York: Random House, Vintage Books, 1967.

CAROTHERS, J. C. *The African Mind in Health and Disease: A Study in Ethnopsychiatry.* Geneva: World Health Organization Monograph Series, No. 17, 1953.

CAUTE, DAVID. *Fanon.* London: Fontana/Collins, 1970.

CÉSAIRE, AIMÉ. *Discourse on Colonialism.* New York: Monthly Review Press, 1972.

CLEAVER, ELDRIDGE. *Soul on Ice.* New York: Dell, 1968.

COLEMAN, JAMES S. *Nigeria: Background to Nationalism.* Berkeley and Los Angeles: University of California Press, 1958.

CROWDER, MICHAEL. *Senegal: A Study in French Assimilation Policy.* London: Oxford University Press, 1962.

CRUSE, HAROLD. *The Crisis of the Negro Intellectual.* New York: William Morrow, 1967.

DAVIDSON, BASIL. *The Liberation of Guiné.* Harmondsworth, Middlesex: Penguin Books, 1969.

DEBRAY, RÉGIS. *Revolution in the Revolution?* New York: Grove Press, 1967.

DE GEORGE, RICHARD T. *Ethics and Society.* Garden City, N.Y.: Doubleday, 1966.

DEKADT, EMANUEL. *Patterns of Foreign Influence in the Caribbean.* London: Oxford University Press, 1972.

DESAN, WILFORD. *The Tragic Finale: An Essay on the Philosophy of Jean-Paul Sartre.* Cambridge, Mass.: Harvard University Press, 1954.

DIKE, ONWUKA K. *Trade and Politics in the Niger Delta, 1830–1885.* Oxford: Clarendon Press, 1956.

DJOLETO, AMU. *The Strange Man.* London: Heinemann, 1967.

DUMONT, RENÉ. *False Start in Africa.* London: André Deutsch, 1966.

EMERY, LYNNE F. *Black Dance in the United States from 1619 to 1970.* Palo Alto, Calif.: National Press, 1972.

FEUER, LEWIS S. *Marx and Engels: Basic Writings on Politics and Philosophy.* Garden City, N.Y.: Doubleday, 1959.

FINKLE, JASON L., and RICHARD W. GABLE. *Political Development and Social Change.* New York: John Wiley, 1968.

FITCH, BOB, and MARY OPPENHEIMER. *Ghana: End of an Illusion.* New York: Monthly Review Press, 1966.

FRAZIER, E. FRANKLIN. *Black Bourgeoisie.* New York: Macmillan, Collier Books, 1962.

FYFE, CHRISTOPHER. *Africanus Horton.* Oxford and New York: Oxford University Press, 1972.

GEISMAR, PETER. *Fanon.* New York: Dial Press, 1971.

GELLNER, ERNEST, and GHITA IONESCU. *Populism: Its Meaning and National Characteristics.* London: Macmillan, 1969.

MOSS, WARNER. *Violence*. Williamsburg, Va.: College of William and Mary in Virginia, 1968.

MURCH, ARVIN. *Black Frenchmen: The Political Integration of the French Antilles*. Cambridge, Mass.: Schenkman, 1971.

NISBET, ROBERT. *The Social Philosophers*. New York: Thomas Y. Crowell, 1973.

NKRUMAH, KWAME. *Class Struggle in Africa*. New York: International Publishers, 1970.

———. *Consciencism*. New York: Monthly Review Press, 1970.

———. *Handbook of Revolutionary Warfare*. New York: International Publishers, 1969.

NYERERE, JULIUS K. *Uhuru Na Ujamaa: Freedom and Socialism*. New York: Oxford University Press, 1968.

———. *Ujamaa: Essays on Socialism*. Dar-es-Salaam: Oxford University Press, 1968.

ODAJNYK, WALTER. *Marxism and Existentialism*. Garden City, N.Y.: Doubleday, 1965.

OLLMAN, BERTELL. *Alienation: Marx's Conception of Man in Capitalist Society*. Cambridge: At the University Press, 1971.

OTTAWAY, DAVID, and MARINA OTTAWAY. *Algeria: The Politics of a Socialist Revolution*. Berkeley and Los Angeles: University of California Press, 1970.

OYONO, FERDINAND. *The Old Man and the Medal*. Translated by John Reed. New York: Macmillan, Collier Books, 1971.

POUSSAINT, ALVIN F. *Why Blacks Kill Blacks*. New York: Emerson Hall Publishers, 1972.

PYZIUR, EUGENE. *The Doctrine of Anarchism of Michael A. Bakunin*. Chicago: Henry Regnery, 1968.

QUANDT, WILLIAM B. *Revolution and Political Leadership: Algeria, 1954-1968*. Cambridge, Mass.: M.I.T. Press, 1969.

REJAI, M. *Mao Tse-tung on Revolution and War*. Garden City, N.Y.: Doubleday, 1970.

RIGGS, FRED W. *Administration in Developing Countries*. Boston: Houghton Mifflin, 1964.

ROSBERG, CARL G., Jr., and JOHN NOTTINGHAM. *The Myth of "Mau Mau": Nationalism in Kenya*. Nairobi: East African Publishing House, 1966.

ROSS, A. M., ed. *Industrial Relations and Economic Development*. London: Macmillan, 1966.

ROUSSEAU, JEAN-JACQUES. *The Social Contract and Discourse on the Origin of Inequality*. Edited by Lester Crocker. New York: Washington Square Press, 1967.

SARTRE, JEAN-PAUL. *Black Orpheus*. Paris: Présence Africaine, n.d.

———. *Critique de la raison dialectique*. Paris: Gallimard, 1960.

———. *Iron in the Soul*. London: Hamish Hamilton, 1950.

Seale, Bobby. *Seize the Time*. New York: Random House, Vintage Books, 1970.

Schram, Stuart R. *The Political Thought of Mao Tse-Tung*. New York: Praeger, 1969.

SCHACHT, RICHARD. *Alienation*. Garden City, N.Y.: Doubleday, 1971.

SEMBENE, OUSMANE. *God's Bits of Wood*. Translated by Francis Price. Garden City, N.Y.: Doubleday, 1970.

SHAFFER, JEROME A. *Violence*. New York: David McKay, 1971.

SHAMUYARIRA, M. N. *Essays on the Liberation of Southern Africa*. Dar-es-Salaam: Tanzania Publishing House, Studies in Political Science, No. 3, 1971.

SHANIN, TEODOR. *Peasants and Peasant Societies*. Harmondsworth, Middlesex: Penguin, 1971.

SHIVJI, ISSA G. *The Silent Class Struggle Continues*. Dar-es-Salaam: Tanzania Publishing House, 1973.

SOREL, GEORGES. *Reflections on Violence*. New York: Macmillan, Collier Books, 1961.

TROTSKY, LEON. *Literature and Revolution*. New York: International Publishers, 1925.

VENYŠ, LADISLAV. *A History of the Mau Mau Movement in Kenya*. Prague: Charles University, 1970.

WEINSTEIN, BRIAN. *Éboué*. New York: Oxford University Press, 1972.

WERTHEIM, W. F. *Evolution and Revolution*. Harmondsworth, Middlesex: Penguin, 1974.

WILLIAMS, ERIC. *Capitalism and Slavery*. New York: G. P. Putnam's Sons, Capricorn Books, 1966.

WODDIS, JACK. *New Theories of Revolution*. New York: International Publishers, 1972.

WOLF, ERIC R. *Peasant Wars of the Twentieth Century*. London: Farber & Farber, 1971.

———. *Peasants*. Englewood Cliffs, N.J.: Prentice-Hall, 1966.

WOLFENSTEIN, VICTOR E. *The Revolutionary Personality: Lenin, Trotsky, Ghandi*. Princeton, N.J.: Princeton University Press, 1971.

WOLFF, ROBERT PAUL, et al. *A Critique of Pure Tolerance*. Boston: Beacon Press, 1969.

WRIGHT, RICHARD. *Native Son*. New York: New American Library, 1964.

YETMAN, NORMAN, and HOY STEELE. *Majority and Minority: The Dynamics of Racial and Ethnic Relations*. Boston: Allyn & Beacon, 1971.

ZAHAR, RENATE. *L'Oeuvre de Frantz Fanon. Paris:* François Maspéro, 1970.

ARTICLES

ABEL, LIONEL. "Seven Heroes of the New Left." *New York Times Magazine*, 5 May 1968, pp. 30–31, 128–33, 135.

ABRASH, BARBARA. "Frantz Fanon: Bio-bibliography." *Africana Library Journal* 11 (Autumn 1971): 9–12.

———. "Fanon: Political Philosopher as Mythmaker." In Emmanuel Hansen and Adele Jinadu, eds. *Frantz Fanon: The Man, His Work, and His Thought*. Forthcoming.

ADAM, HUSSEIN MOHAMED. "Frantz Fanon: His 'Understanding.' " *Black World* 21 (December 1971): 4–14.

ADAMS, PAUL L. "The Social Psychiatry of Frantz Fanon." *American Journal of Psychiatry* 127 (December 1970): 109–14.

AFRICANUS, POLYBIUS. "Frantz Fanon's Essays." *Liberation* 12 (August 1967): 34–35.

ALAVI, HAMZA. "Peasants and Revolutions." *Socialist Register*, 1965, pp. 241–77.

ALLEN, CHRIS. " 'Lumpen-proletarians' and Revolution." In *Political Theory and Ideology in African Society*. Edinburgh: Centre for African Studies, 1970.

ALSOP, JOSEPH. Letter to *New Statesman*, 30 January 1970, p. 150.

———. "Passing of New Left's Hero: An Odd Facet of U.S. History." *Washington Post*, 21 February 1969, p. 21.

AMGHAR, MOHAMMED. "Fanon et la pensée occidentale." *El Moudjahid*, 2 June 1971, pp. 4–5.

AMIN, SAMIR. "The Class Struggle in Africa." Africa Research Group (Cambridge, Mass.), n.d.

ANSPRENGER, FRANZ. Review of *Les Damnés de la terre. Journal of Modern African Studies* 1 (1963): 403–5.

ARENDT, HANNAH. "Reflections on Violence." *New York Review of Books* 12 (February 1969): 19–31.

Armah, Ayi Kwei. "Fanon: The Awakener." *Negro Digest* 18 (October 1969): 4-9, 29-43.

Arrighi, Giovanni, and John Saul. "Nationalism and Revolution in Sub-Saharan Africa." *Socialist Register*, 1969, pp. 137-88.

Bailby, Edouard. "Les Risques du tout ou rien." *L'Express*, No. 1037 (24-30 May 1971), pp. 20-21.

Barnard, Roger. "Frantz Fanon." *New Society*, 4 January 1968, pp. 11-13.

Becket, Paul A. "Algeria vs. Fanon: The Theory of Revolutionary Decolonization and the Algerian Experience." *Western Political Quarterly* 26 (March 1973): 5-27.

———. "Frantz Fanon and Sub-Saharan Africa: Notes on the Contemporary Significance of His Thought." *Africa Today* 19 (Spring 1972): 59-73.

Bell, Daniel. "The Rediscovery of Alienation." *Journal of Philosophy* 56 (19 November 1959): 933-52.

Blackey, Robert. "Fanon and Cabral: A Contrast in Theories of Revolution for Africa." *Journal of Modern African Studies* 12 (June 1974): 191-209.

Bondy, François. "Frantz Fanon." *Encounter* 53 (August 1974): pp. 25-29.

———. "The Black Rousseau." *New York Review of Books*, 31 March 1966.

Breitman, George. Review of *The Wretched of the Earth*. *Militant*, 27 September 1965.

Bronfenbrenner, Martin. "A Harder Look at Alienation." *Ethics* 83 (July 1973): 267-82.

Bundy, Colin. "Emergence and Decline of a South African Peasantry." *African Affairs*, No. 285 (October 1972), pp. 369-88.

Capouya, Emile. "Time to Turn a Tide of Violence." *Saturday Review*, 24 April 1965, pp. 33-34.

Caute, David. "Philosopher of Violence." *Observer*, 10 October 1965, p. 26.

Césaire, Aimé. "La Révolte de Frantz Fanon." *Jeune Afrique*, No. 63 (13-19 December 1961), pp. 24-25.

———. "M. Césaire déclare à L'Express." *L'Express*, No. 1037 (24-30 May 1971), pp. 20-21.

Cherif, Mohamed. "Frantz Fanon: la Science au service de la révolution." *Jeune Afrique*, No. 295 (4 September 1966), p. 24.

Chodak, Szymon. "The Birth of an African Peasantry." *Canadian Journal of African Studies* Vol. 5, No. 3 (1971), pp. 327-47.

———. "Social Classes in Sub-Saharan Africa." *Africana Bulletin*, No. 4 (1966), pp. 7-46.

———. "Social Stratification in Sub-Saharan Africa." *Canadian Journal of African Studies*, Vol. 7, No. 3 (1973), pp. 401–17.

CLAPHAM, CHRISTOPHER. "The Context of African Political Thought." *Journal of Modern African Studies* 8 (April 1970): 1–13.

COHEN, ROBIN. "Class in Africa: Analytical Problems and Perspectives." *Socialist Register*, 1972, pp. 231–55.

COHEN, ROBIN, and DAVID MICHAEL. "The Revolutionary Potential of the African Lumpenproletariat: A Sceptical View." *Bulletin of the Institute of Development Studies* (Sussex University), Vol. 5, Nos. 2-3 (1973), pp. 31–42.

COLES, ROBERT. "Abused and Abusers." *New York Times Book Review*, 30 April 1967, p. 3.

———. "What Colonialism Does." *New Republic*, 18 September 1965, pp. 20, 22, 23.

COSER, LEWIS. "Fanon and Debray: Theorists of the Third World." In Irving Howe, ed., *Beyond the New Left*, pp. 120–34. New York: McCall Publishing Co., 1970.

CRANSTON, MAURICE. "Sartre and Violence: A Philosopher's Commitment to a Pledge." *Encounter* 29 (July 1967): 18–24.

CZARNECKI, JAN. "Un Livre révolutionnaire: Les Damnés de la terre." *Christianisme sociale*, 1963, pp. 176–84.

DANIEL, JEAN. "Fanon, un 'Piednoir' et le Gaullisme." *L'Express*, 14 December 1961, p. 17.

———. Review of *Les Damnés de la terre*. *L'Express*, 30 November 1961, p. 36.

DAVIDSON, BASIL. "African Peasants and Revolution." *Journal of Peasant Studies* 1 (April 1974): 269–90.

DEMING, BARBARA. "On Revolution and Equilibrium." *Liberation* 12 (February 1968): 10–21.

DIENG, AMADY ALY. "Les Damnés de la terre et les problèmes d'Afrique noire." *Présence Africaine*, No. 62 (1967), pp. 15–30.

DOMENACH, JEAN-MARIE. Review of *Les Damnés de la terre*. *Esprit*, No. 304 (March 1962), pp. 454–63.

DUBOIS, FRANÇOISE. Review of *Pour la révolution africaine*. *Tiers monde* 5 (July-September 1964): 595–56.

EPSTEIN, DAVID G. "A Revolutionary Lumpenproletariat." *Monthly Review*, December 1969, pp. 54–56.

Fabre, Geneviève et Kessous. "Frantz Fanon et la rêvolte noire." *Le Monde diplomatique*, December 1971.

Fallers, L. A. "Are African Cultivators to Be Called 'Peasants'?" *Current Anthropology*, Vol. 2, No. 2 (1961), pp. 108–10.

Fanon, Josie. "A propos de Frantz Fanon, Sartre, le racisme, et les arabes." *El Moudjahid*, 10 June 1967, p. 6.

Feuer, Lewis. "What Is Alienation? The Career of a Concept." *New Politics* 1 (Spring 1962): 116–34.

Finlay, David. "Students and Politics in Ghana." *Daedalus* 97 (Winter 1968): 51–69.

Forsythe, Dennis. "Frantz Fanon: Black Theoretician." *Black Scholar* 1 (March 1970): 3–10.

Franklin, Bruce. "The Lumpen proletariat and the Revolutionary Youth Movement." *Monthly Review* 21 (January 1970): 10–25.

Freeman, Michael. "Review Article: Theories of Revolution." *British Journal of Political Science* 2 (1972): 339–59.

Furedi, Frank. "The Social Composition of the 'Mau Mau' Movement in the White Highlands." *Journal of Peasant Studies* 1 (July 1974): 486–505.

Geismar, Peter. "Frantz Fanon: Evolution of a Revolutionary. A Biographical Sketch." *Monthly Review* 21 (May 1969): 22–30.

Gendzier, Irene. "Frantz Fanon: In Search of Justice." *Middle East Journal* 20 (Autumn 1966): 534–44.

———. "Frantz Fanon: From Psychiatry to Political Action." Paper presented at the Fifteenth Annual Meeting of the African Studies Association, Philadelphia, 8–11 November 1972.

———. "Reflections on Fanon and the Jewish Question." *New Outlook* 12 (January 1969): 13–20.

Gert, Bernard. "On Violence." *Journal of Philosophy* 66 (1969): 616–28.

Gleason, Ralph J. "An Introduction to Frantz Fanon." *Ramparts* 4 (March 1966): 36–38.

Goldman, Lawrence. "Fanon and Black Radicalism." *Monthly Review* 18 (November 1966): 50–58.

Gordon, David. "Frantz Fanon: Voice of the Algerian Revolution." *Middle East Forum*, September 1963, pp. 17–20.

Gottheil Fred M. "Fanon and the Economics of Colonialism: A Review Article." *Quarterly Review of Economics and Business* 7 (Autumn 1967): 73–82.

GREKI, ANNA. "Les Damnés de la terre." *Jeune Afrique*, No. 63 (13–19 December 1961), p. 25.

GRUNDY, KENNETH. "The 'Class Struggle' in Africa: An Examination of Conflicting Theories." *Journal of Modern African Studies* 2 (November 1964): 379–93.

GUTKIND, PETER C. W. "The Energy of Despair: Social Organization of the Unemployed in Two African Cities: Lagos and Nairobi." *Civilisations*, Vol. 17, No. 3 (1967), pp. 186–211; Vol. 17, No. 4 (1967), pp. 380–402.

HAAG, ERNEST. Review of *The Wretched of the Earth. Modern Age* 10 (Spring 1966): 184–86.

HACKER, SUSAN. "Violent and Non-Violent Approaches to Revolution." *Mawaso* 3 (June 1972): 1–11.

HALE, DENNIS. Review of *The Wretched of the Earth. Motive* 26 (January 1966): 52–53.

HANSEN, EMMANUEL. "Frantz Fanon: A Bibliographical Essay." *Pan-African Journal* 5 (Winter 1972): 387–405.

———. "Frantz Fanon: Portrait of a Revolutionary Intellectual." *Transition*, No. 46 (October-December 1974), pp. 25–36.

HARRIS, WILLIAM. "Manuals for Black Militants." *Antioch Review* 37 (November 1967): 408–16.

HATCH, STEPHEN. "Coloured People in School Textbooks." *Race* 4 (November 1962): 63–72.

HATTO, ARTHUR. "Revolution: An Inquiry into the Usefulness of an Historical Term." *Mind* 58 (1949): 495–517.

HENTOFF, NAT. "Bursting into History." *New Yorker*, 15 January 1965, pp. 115–17.

HERMASSI, ABDELBAKE. "L'Idéologie Fanonienne." *Jeune Afrique*, No. 295 (4 September 1966), p. 25.

HINCHLIFFE, KEITH. "Labour Aristocracy—A Northern Nigerian Case Study." *Journal of Modern African Studies* 12 (March 1974): 57–67.

HILL, POLLY. "The Myth of the Amorphous Peasantry: A Northern Nigerian Case Study." *Nigerian Journal of Economic and Social Studies* 10 (July 1968): 239–60.

Homages to Frantz Fanon, *Présence Africaine*, Vol. 12, No. 40 (1962), pp. 130–52.

HOROWITZ, IRVING LOUIS. "On Alienation and the Social Order." *Philosophy and Phenomenological Research* 27 (December 1966): 230–37.

HYDEN, G. "The Failure of Africa's First Intellectuals." *Transition* 6 (January 1967): 14–18.

ILLUNGA-KABONGO, ANDRÉ. "Les Damnés de la terre." In Joseph Okpaku, ed., *New African Literature and the Arts*, 1:91–96. New York: Thomas Y. Crowell.

IRELE, ABIOLA. "Literature and Ideology in Martinique: René Maran, Aimé Césaire, Frantz Fanon." *Research Review*, Vol. 5, No. 3, Trinity Term (Ghana University, Institute of African Studies, 1969), pp. 1–32.

———. "Negritude or Black Cultural Nationalism." *Journal of Modern African Studies*, Vol. 3, No. 3 (1965), pp. 321–48.

———. "Negritude Revisited." *Odu: A Journal of West African Studies*, No. 5, n.s. (April 1971), pp. 3–26.

ISAACS, HAROLD R. "Portrait of a Revolutionary." *Commentary* 40 (July 1965): 67–71.

JACKSON, HENRY. "Political and Social Ideas of Frantz Fanon: Relevance to Black Americans." *Pan-African Journal* 5 (Winter 1974): 473–91.

JACKSON, R. H. "Political Stratification in Tropical Africa." *Canadian Journal of African Studies*, Vol. 7, No. 3 (1973), pp. 381–400.

JINADU, ADELE L. "On the Notion of 'Deficiency' in Frantz Fanon." Paper presented at the Fifteenth Annual Meeting of the African Studies Association, Philadelphia, 8–11 November 1972.

———. "Some Aspects of the Political Philosophy of Frantz Fanon." *Pan-African Journal* 5 (Winter 1972): 493–522; also *African Studies Review* 16 (September 1973): 255–89.

———. "Some Comments on Frantz Fanon and the Historiography of African Politics." *Journal of Developing Areas* 7 (January 1973): 287–97.

JOHNS, SHERIDAN. "Obstacles to Guerrilla Warfare: A South African Case Study." *Journal of Modern African Studies* 11 (June 1973): 267–303.

JONES, JOHN HENRY. "On the Influence of Fanon." *Freedomways* 8 (Summer 1968): 209–14.

KABWEGYERE, TARSIS. "The Dynamics of Colonial Violence: The Inductive System in Uganda." *Journal of Peace Research*, No. 4 (1972), pp. 303–14.

KAMENJU, GRANT. "Frantz Fanon." *Transition* 26 (1966): 51–52.

KAMENKA, EUGENE. "The Concept of a Political Revolution." In Carl Friedrich, ed., *Revolution*, pp. 122–35. New York: Atherton, 1966.

KAPLINSKY, RAPHAEL. "Myths about the 'Revolutionary Proletariat' in Developing Countries." *Bulletin of the Institute of Development Studies* (Sussex University) 3 (August 1971): 15–21.

KAUFMAN, ARNOLD S. "On Alienation." *Inquiry* 8 (Summer 1965): 141–65.

KLEIN, NORMAN A. "On Revolutionary Violence." *Studies on the Left* 4 (May-June 1966): 62–82.

KNIGHT, VERE W. "Fanon: The View from the Colonies." *Black Images* 2 (Spring 1973): 16–20.

KRAMNIC, ISAAC. "Reflections on Revolution: Definition and Explanation in Recent Scholarship." *History and Theory: Studies in Philosophy of History*, Vol. 11, No. 1 (1972), pp. 26–63.

KRÉA, HENRI. "Verités premières." in Denise Barrat, ed., *Espoir et parole*, pp. 85–88. Paris: Seghers, 1963.

KUPER. LEO. "Theories of Revolution and Race Relations." *Comparative Studies in Society and History* 13 (January 1971): 87–107.

LASKY, MELVIN J. "The Birth of a Metaphor." *Encounter* 34 (February 1970): 35–45; 34 (March 1970): 30–42.

LEDDA, ROMANO. "Social Class and Political Struggle." *International Socialist Journal*, No. 22 (August 1967), pp. 560–80.

LEWIS, MARTIN DEMING. "One Hundred Million Frenchmen: The 'Assimilation' Theory in French Colonial Policy." *Comparative Studies in Society and History* 4 (January 1962): 129–53.

LEYS, COLIN. "Politics in Kenya: The Development of Peasant Society." *British Journal of Political Science* 1 (July 1971): 307–37.

LOFCHIE, MICHAEL. "The Uganda Coup: Class Action by the Military." *Journal of Modern African Studies* 10 (May 1972): 19–35.

———. "Political Origins of the Uganda Coup." *Journal of African Studies* 1 (Winter 1974): 464–96.

LONG, RICHARD. "Negritude: Philosophy of Culture." In Walter D. Abilla, ed., *Source Book in Black Studies*, pp. 74–86. New York: MSS Information, 1972.

LOWENTHAL, DAVID. "Race and Color in the West Indies." *Daedalus*, Spring, 1967.

MAINBERGER, GONSALV. "A la mêmoire de Frantz Fanon: mythe et réalité de l'homme noir." *Présence Africaine* 46 (1963), pp. 79–92.

MALABRE, ALFRED L., Jr. "A Disturbing Diatribe from the 'Third World.' " *Wall Street Journal*, 23 July 1965, p. 8.

MAQUET, JACQUES J. "La Participation de la classe paysanne au Mouvement d'Indépendance de Rwanda." *Cahiers d'études africaines*, Vol. 4, No. 16 (1964), pp. 552–68.

MARCUSE, HERBERT. "Ethics and Revolution." In Richard T. De George, ed., *Ethics and Society*, pp. 133–47. Garden City, N.Y.: Doubleday, 1966.

MARTIN, GUY. "Fanon's Relevance to Contemporary African Political Thought." *Ufahamu* 4 (Winter 1974): 11–34.

MARTIN, TONY. "Rescuing Fanon from the Critics." *African Studies Review* 13 (December 1970): 381–99.

MARTIN-KANE, GUY. "Fanon on Violence and the Revolutionary Process in Africa." *African Insight* 2 (1974): 14–19.

MASCHINO, MAURICE. "Frantz Fanon: L'Itinéraire de la générosité." *Partisans*, February 1962, pp. 5–15.

MAZRUI, ALI. "The Lumpen Proletariat and the Lumpen Militariat: African Soldiers as a New Political Class." *Political Studies* 21 (March 1973): 1–12.

MEMMI, ALBERT. "Frantz Fanon and the Notion of 'Deficiency.' " In Albert Memmi, *Dominated Man*, pp. 84–89. New York: Orion Press, 1968.

———. "La Vie impossible de Frantz Fanon." *Esprit*, September 1971, pp. 248–73.

———. "Frozen by Death in the Image of Third World Prophet." *New York Times Book Review*, 14 May 1971, pp. 5, 20.

M'HAMSADJI, KADDOUR. "Sociologie de Frantz Fanon." *El Moudjahid*, 14 January 1972.

MILI, M. MOHAMMED EL. "Frantz Fanon et la Révolution Algérienne." *El Moudjahid*, 20 March, 1971, p. 3.

———. "Fanon et la pensée occidentale." *El Moudjahid*, 2 June 1971.

MOHAN, JITENDRA. "Nkrumah and Nkrumaism." *Socialist Register*, 1967, pp. 191–228.

MOHIDDIN, AHMAD. "Nyerere and Fanon on African Development and Leadership." *Pan-African Journal* 6 (Summer 1973): 163-208.

MORGENTHAU, RUTH SCHACHTER. "Frantz Fanon: Five Years Later." *Africa Report*, May 1966, pp. 69–71.

MUSEVENI, YOWERI T. "Fanon's Theory of Violence: Its Verification in Liberated Mozambique." In Nathan Shamuyarira, ed., *Essays on the Liberation of Southern Africa*, pp. 1–24. Dar-es-Salaam: Tanzania Publishing, 1971.

MULAMBU-MVULUYA, F. "Introduction à l'étude du rôle des paysans dans les changements politiques." *Cahiers économiques et sociaux* 8 (September 1970): 435–50.

NGHE, NGUYEN. "Frantz Fanon et les problèmes de l'indépendance." *La Pensée*, No. 107 (February 1963), pp. 23-36.

NKRUMAH, KWAME. "African Socialism Revisited." *African Forum* 1 (Winter 1966): 3–9.

NURSEY-BRAY, PAUL. "Marxism and Existentialism in the Thought of Frantz Fanon." *Political Studies* 20 (June 1972): 152–68.

NZONGALA, GEORGES N. "Les classes sociales et la révolution anticolonial au Congo-Kinshasa: le rôle de la bourgeoisie." *Cahiers économiques et sociaux* 8 (September 1970): 371–88.

OBIECHINA, EMMANUEL. "Frantz Fanon: The Man and His Works." *Ufahamu* 3 (Fall 1972): 97–116.

O'BRIEN, CONOR CRUISE. "The Neurosis of Colonialism." *Nation* 200 (June 1965): 674–76.

OLORUNSOLA, VICTOR A., and RAMAKRIS VAITHESWARAN. "Reflections Prompted by Frantz Fanon's *The Wretched of the Earth*: A Review Essay." *Journal of Developing Areas* 5 (October 1971): 123-26.

PABLO, MICHEL. "Les Damnés de la terre." *Quatrième internationale* 20 (February 1962): 57–63.

PARIS, ROBERT. "Sur un premier bilan du 'Fanonisme.' " *Partisans*, No. 8 (January-February 1963), pp. 177–85.

PAUTARD, ANDRÉ. "La Mémoire de Frantz Fanon (M. Ben Bella rappelle aux algériens les exigences d'une politique d'austérité." *Le Monde*, 27 December 1962.

PEIL, MARGARET. "The Ghanaian University Students: The Broadening Base." *British Journal of Sociology* 16 (March 1965): 19–28.

PERINBAM, B. MARIE. "Fanon and the Revolutionary Peasantry: The Algerian Case." *Journal of Modern African Studies* 2 (September 1973): 427–45.

POUILLON, JEAN. "Décolonisation et révolution." *Les Temps modernes*, No. 191 (April 1962), pp. 1554-63.

POSINSKY, S. H. Review of *The Wretched of the Earth* and *Studies in a Dying Colonialism. Psychoanalytic Quarterly* 35 (1966): 600-602.

QUELLE, CHARIF. "Frantz Fanon and Colonized Man." *Africa Today* 17 (January-February 1970): 8–11.

———. "Frantz Fanon: Prophet of Revolution." *Washington Post*, 2 August 1971, pp. B1, B6.

RANLY, ERNEST W. "Frantz Fanon and the Radical Left." *America* 121 (November 1969): 384, 387–88.

SAUL, JOHN. "African Peasants and Revolution." *Review of African Political Economy*, No. 1 (1974), pp. 41–68.

SAUL, JOHN, and ROGER WOODS. "African Peasantries." In Teodor Shanin, ed., *Peasants and Peasant Societies*, pp. 103–14. Harmondsworth, Middlesex: Penguin, 1971.

SCHAFF, ADAM. "Marxist Theory on Revolution and Violence." *Journal of the History of Ideas* 34 (April-June 1973): 263–70.

SCHAPIRO, LEONARD. "A Lost Politics." *New York Review of Books*, 5 December 1968, pp. 25–30.

SEIGEL, J. E. "On Frantz Fanon." *American Scholar* 38 (Winter 1968): 84–96.

SENGHOR, L. "Negritude and the Concept of Universal Civilization." *Prêsence Africaine* 18 (Second Quarter, 1963): 9–13.

SMITH, ROBERT. "Beyond Marx: Fanon and the Concept of Colonial Violence." *Black World*, May 1973, pp. 23–33.

STAMBOULI, F. "Frantz Fanon face aux problèmes de la décolonisation et de la construction nationale." *Institut de sociologie revue* (Brussels Free University) (1967), pp. 519–34.

STANILAND, MARTIN. "Frantz Fanon and the African Political Class." *African Affairs*, January 1969, pp. 4–25.

SUTTON, HORACE. "Fanon." *Saturday Review*, 17 July 1971, pp. 16–19, 59–60.

TALMON, J. L. "The Legacy of Georges Sorel." *Encounter* 34 (February 1970): 47–60.

THOMPSON, WILLIE. "Frantz Fanon." *Marxism Today*, August 1968, pp. 245–51.

TRAORE, BABARY. "On 'Les Damnés de la Terre.' " *Prêsence Africaine*, Vol. 17, No. 45 (1963), pp. 88–95.

VAN DEN BURGHE, PIERRE. "European Languages and Black Mandarins." *Transition* 7 (December-January 1968): 19–23.

WALLERSTEIN, IMMANUEL. "Frantz Fanon: Reason and Violence." *Journal of Sociology* (Berkeley) 15 (1970).

———. "Class and Class Conflict in Contemporary Africa." *Canadian Journal of African Studies*, Vol. 7, No. 3 (1973), pp. 375–80.

———. Review of *Studies in a Dying Colonialism*. *New World Quarterly*, Vol. 3, No. 3 (1967), pp. 76–77.

WATERMAN, PETER. "Conservatism among Nigerian Workers: A Contribution to the Debate on Africa's 'Labour Aristocracy.' " The Hague: Institute of Social Studies, mimeo., June 1974.

———. "The 'Labour Aristocracy' in Africa: An Introduction to a Debate." The Hague: Institute of Social Studies, mimeo., n.d.

WILLIAMS, GAVIN. "The Social Stratification of a Neo-Colonial Economy." In Christopher Allen and R. W. Johnson, eds., *African Perspectives*, pp. 225–50. Cambridge: At the University Press, 1970.

WOLFF, ROBERT PAUL. "On Violence." *Journal of Philosophy* 66 (1969): 601–16.

WORSLEY, PETER. "Revolutionary Theories." *Monthly Review* 21 (May 1969): 30–49.

———. "The Coming Inheritors." *Guardian*, 22 October 1965.

———. "Frantz Fanon and the 'Lumpenproletariat.' " *Socialist Register*, 1972, pp. 193–230.

ZAGORIN, PAREZ. "Theories of Revolution in Contemporary Historiography." *Political Science Quarterly* 88 (March 1973): 23–52.

ZOLBERG, ARISTIDE, and VERA ZOLBERG. "The Americanization of Frantz Fanon." *Public Interest*, No. 9 (1969), pp. 49–63.

ZOLBERG, ARISTIDE R. "Frantz Fanon: A Gospel for the Damned." *Encounter* 27 (November 1966): 56–63.

index